Endorsements

The *Praying with Jesus* resource is intended to serve the National Prayer Accord in a rhythm of prayer for spiritual awakening (see page back pages of this book for more information about the National Prayer Accord). This growing heart-cry for spiritual awakening has been adopted by denominational and parachurch leaders from across the faith community. The Denominational Prayer Leaders Network is one of these supportive groups and includes prayer leaders such as Claude King and P. Douglas Small. Read their encouragement below.

Genuine prayer is not a religious ritual for Christians to practice a few times each day. Prayer is a relationship God has with His children in which we talk with our heavenly Father. Prayer is a time for us to enter the presence of the Creator and Ruler of the universe to understand what is on His mind and heart. Prayer is a holy privilege made possible by the sacrifice of Jesus Christ on our behalf.

When God calls His people to return to Him and they respond in repentance and united prayer, God is able to bring the revival He desires of us. When God's people begin to pray for the kingdom work of bringing the lost to Christ, God calls many as laborers in His harvest. Our nation and the world have reached a desperate point, and again we need to hear God's call to explicit agreement through visible union in extraordinary prayer. Let's learn to pray together and join God's work of transforming our nation and our world for His glory.

Claude King
Discipleship Specialist, Lifeway

God is calling us to pray with persistence toward His purposes being fulfilled in our communities in our generation. It is no longer sufficient to pray transactional prayers with a focus on emergencies and momentary needs. Narcissistic praying is inevitably boring. The small victories won in narrow self-interested praying pale in comparison to the transformational power of prayer that changes us, our families and churches, as well as whole communities. God is inviting us to join Him in cosmic purposes that have an eternal impact. If we respond to the call, we will discover ourselves in the midst of the once-in-history finishing of the Great Commission, in the spirit of the Great Commandment, out of the energy of prayer, the Great Commitment.

P. Douglas Small
National Prayer Coordinator, Church of God

Published by BroadStreet Publishing Group, LLC
Racine, Wisconsin, USA
www.broadstreetpublishing.com

PRAYING WITH *Jesus*
○ R=S=T *My Prayer Life*

ISBN: 978-1-4245-5121-7 (hard cover)
ISBN: 978-1-4245-5122-4 (e-book)

This title may be purchased in bulk for ministry purposes. For information go to the online store at www.greatcommandment.net or call 800-881-8008.

Cover by Chris Garborg at www.garborgdesign.com
Interior by Kimberly Sagmiller at www.fudgecreative.com

Printed in China

15 16 17 18 19 20 5 4 3 2 1

SPIRIT-
EMPOWERED
Faith

PRAYING
WITH
Jesus

 RESET

My Prayer Life

BroadStreet
PUBLISHING

Contents

SECTION 1:

A Spirit-empowered faith means that I will love the Lord through practicing the presence of Jesus and yielding to the Spirit's work of Christlikeness.

SECTION 2:

A Spirit-empowered faith means that I will love the Word through being a "living epistle" in reverence and awe as His Word becomes real in my life, vocation, and calling.

SECTION 3:

A Spirit-empowered faith will mean that I love people by ministering Christ's life and love to my nearest ones at home and with family, as well as faithful engagement in His Body, the church.

SECTION 4:

A Spirit-empowered faith will mean that I love His mission through expressing and extending the kingdom of God as compassion, justice, love, and forgiveness are shared.

SECTION 5:

A Spirit-empowered faith will mean that I love His mission through pouring life into others and making disciples who, in turn, make disciples of others.

APPENDIX:

WHY PRAY WITH JESUS?

Since the earliest days of European interest in the Americas, God's people have sought a place to worship in freedom and longed to experience spiritual awakening. Along the way, God has chosen a variety of places and people to awaken the nation for Christ: the colonial village of Northampton, Massachusetts; the Cane Ridge Camp Meeting; New York City's Bowery district; a renovated livery stable on 312 Azusa Street in Los Angeles; and your world. You are a vital link to the next great awakening looming on the horizon of America in our generation.

Each occurrence of nationwide revival has been different, yet one common denominator has always been evident: a sense of hungry, prayerful desperation. Each time the extended masses have humbled themselves and sought God's deliverance, He has responded in power. That is why in the midst of obvious spiritual decline across America, we have reason for hope today.

In 2008, an Awakening America Alliance leadership summit was called to reflect on the First Great Awakening and the potential for a contemporary nationwide transformation. Recognizing that true awakenings bring visible change, twenty indicators of awakening were identified and now serve as an evaluation tool for awakening in America.

This resource is structured so that your prayer moments will coincide with each of these twenty indicators. Jesus cares about these topics; He prayed they would be true of us, so let's join Him in prayer.

Joining Jesus in prayer is a part of a Spirit-empowered faith, which moves beyond seeking to simply know or obey the truth.

Actually experiencing truth in our relationship with Jesus will lead us into a relational faith.

In order to fully illustrate what a relational faith includes, we have defined forty different Spirit-empowered outcomes. *Praying with Jesus* is designed with a focus on five of these Spirit-empowered outcomes:

1. A Spirit-empowered faith means that I will love the Lord through practicing the presence of Jesus and yielding to the Spirit's work of Christlikeness.

2. A Spirit-empowered faith means that I will love the Word through being a "living epistle" in reverence and awe as His Word becomes real in my life, vocation, and calling.

3. A Spirit-empowered faith means that I will love people by ministering Christ's life and love to my nearest ones at home and with family, as well as faithful engagement in His body, the church.

4. A Spirit-empowered faith means that I will love His mission through expressing and extending the kingdom of God as compassion, justice, love, and forgiveness are shared.

5. A Spirit-empowered faith means that I will love His mission through pouring life into others and making disciples who, in turn, make disciples of others.

Why pray with Jesus? Because as we agree together in prayer, God can supernaturally bring a divine reversal from darkness to light in the hearts of people who have not experienced His grace. The power of extraordinary, united prayer cannot be overstated. Let's unite our voices with Jesus and experience a Christ awakening in our land!

Kay Horner • Executive Director, Awakening America Alliance
www.awakeningamerica.us

RESET

A PRAYER TO BRING HOPE

RESET YOUR WALK WITH JESUS

When your computer or mobile device freezes, you know to hit the reset button. A reset restores the system to its original design. Hitting "reset" gives it a fresh start. So what happens when it's something in your life that feels frozen? Do you ever wish you could start over? Everyone feels that at times. And Jesus is the reset. Jesus restores you to your original design. He gives you a fresh start. That's what we hope this resource does for your prayer life. May it be a fresh start in your relationship with Jesus!

The *Praying with Jesus* resource is intended to serve the Reset Movement.

Reset is a work of anyone and everyone who wants to see Jesus bring hope to this generation and to this nation. Reset began as a prayer and dream of a young leader from North Dakota named Nick Hall, to see this generation unite around Jesus. The vision was never about one person or organization but a partnership around Jesus—and Jesus calls everyone.

Reset is not an organization. Reset is a prayer and a movement of people sharing the message of the hope Jesus brings when we pray it. The vision is not to facilitate a passive audience, but to catalyze an army of individuals who are actively praying to Jesus to reset their lives, their communities, and their cities—and actively seeking to live a life reset by Jesus. While there are organizations involved, the fuel of this movement is you.

The Reset Movement has identified four ways to start your reset. These four ingredients are the inspiration for calls to action that we have inserted into each of the writings by the authors in this resource.

LEARN to Encounter Jesus

PRAY and Experience Scripture

SHARE with Others in Community

LOVE Others in Community

The message of Reset is that Jesus can and will reset your life. And that same message and invitation is shared at Reset events. The events are a place to connect in person with others who are praying and living reset lives, hear stories of what Jesus is doing, and celebrate Jesus with hundreds and thousands of others who are praying for a Reset. Go to www.resetmovement.com for more information.

Finally, The Great Commandment Network is thrilled to serve each contributor and ministry partner through this resource. Our resource development and training team serves various partners as they develop Spirit-empowered disciples who walk intimately with God's Son, God's Word, and God's people. May Jesus richly bless the unity, commitment, and faith that *Praying with Jesus* represents.

Terri Snead
Executive Editor, Great Commandment Network

The Great Commandment Network is an international collaborative network of strategic kingdom leaders from the faith community, marketplace, education, and caregiving fields who prioritize the powerful simplicity of the words of Jesus to love God, love others, and see others become His followers (Matthew 22:37–40, Matthew 28:19–20).

**"But I (Jesus) have prayed for you (Peter) ...
and when you are restored ... strengthen others."**
(Luke 22:32)

As certainly as Jesus prayed for Peter, He prays for us.

**Jesus Christ is the same yesterday
and today, yes forever.**
(Hebrews 13:8)

And because Jesus never changes, that means He prays for you!

He always lives to make intercession.
(Hebrews 7:25)
Christ Jesus is He ... who also intercedes for us.
(Romans 8:34)

Therefore, the Awakening America Alliance,
The Great Commandment Network, the Reset Movement,
and the Denominational Prayer Leaders Network
would like to join Jesus in prayer for you!

May God strengthen, inspire, and anoint you
to pray in one accord with Him and those He loves.
The power of unity cannot be underestimated!

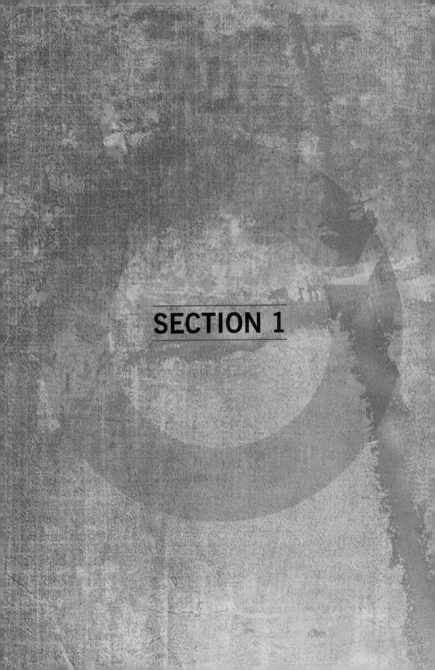

SECTION 1

MY SPIRIT-EMPOWERED FAITH

means that I will love the Lord through practicing the presence of Jesus and yielding to the Spirit's work of Christlikeness.

As I practice this outcome, I will live out the truth that the Lord is with me, for me, speaking to me, and longing to change me.

Listen as He prays for your relationship with God, your love for Him, and His transforming work in your life.

Jesus looked up to heaven and said,
"Father, I have revealed you to them, and I will continue to do so. Then your love for me will be in them, and I will be in them." John 17:26

Now pray with Jesus. Join the prayer meeting that He is already leading on your behalf. *Jesus, please reset my prayer life.*

- I want to experience more and more of Your presence.
- I want to deepen my prayer life and my sensitivity to Your Spirit. I want to become a more faithful disciple of Jesus.
- I want my life to reflect Your principles, truth, and righteousness. I pray that leaders of the church, government, business, and political arenas demonstrate this same righteousness.
- I want to demonstrate the "fear of the Lord" rather than the approval of people. I want to live a life of credibility and integrity.

1

I want to experience more and more of Your presence, Lord.

Jesus, reset my prayer life.

The gospel of John records one of the most intimate prayers of Jesus' life. The night before Christ's death, He vulnerably shared with eleven of His closest friends. Interestingly, it was almost as if Jesus waited for Judas to leave before orchestrating this tender moment. In John 17, we read Jesus' prayer to the Father: "During my time here, I protected them [the disciples] by the power of the name you gave me. I guarded them so that not one was lost, except the one headed for destruction, as the Scriptures foretold" (John 17:12).

Next, the gospel records something amazing! Christ continues to pray for His disciples, but then He prays for you and me!

> I am praying not only for these disciples **but also for all who will ever believe in me** through their message. I pray that they will all be one, just as you and I are one...
>
> John 17:20–21 (emphasis added)

Isn't it amazing to realize that thousands of years before you were born, Jesus prayed for you? He declared that you are His and asked the Father to keep you close. In fact, He asked that we would sense the presence of the Lord so deeply that we would be *in* Jesus.

What will it take for us to experience this kind of closeness?

GOD'S NAME FOR US

From *Forgotten Power: A Simple Theology for a Praying Church*
by Dave Butts*

REMEMBER HIS NAME FOR US

The choosing of a name is very important. We all know parents who agonize over what to name their new baby. Communities often have many meetings and long discussions over how to name a new facility in their town. Biblically, the choosing of a name often gave special significance to a person or place. The name was so important that when there was a change in circumstances, it often meant a name change was necessary.

In Genesis 28, Jacob had an amazing encounter with God in a dream. When he awakened, he renamed the place: "He called the place Bethel, though the city used to be called Luz" (Genesis 28:19). Both Jacob and his father, Abraham, were given name changes by God. In Genesis 17:5, Abram was changed to Abraham and in Genesis 35:10, Jacob became Israel.

Any name is important, regardless of who gives it. But there is special significance when God Himself steps in to name someone or something. That would be especially true when God names something that is particularly close to His heart.

BECOME WHAT HE HAS CALLED US

The Bible tells us that God has chosen a name for His own house. In Isaiah 56:7, the Lord says, "These will I bring to my holy mountain and give them joy in my *house of prayer*. Their burnt offerings and sacrifices will be accepted on my altar; for my house will be called a *house of prayer* for all nations" (emphasis added).

This straightforward naming of the house of God is simply clarifying what God had already declared concerning His house. In the amazing encounter that Solomon had with God at the dedication of the temple, God made it clear that this was to be a place of prayer. Solomon prayed in 2 Chronicles 6:40, "Now, my God, may your eyes be open and your ears attentive to the prayers offered in this place." God's response in 2 Chronicles 7:15 was a resounding yes to that request.

Of great importance to us is the fact that Jesus took this naming seriously. Three of the gospel writers mentioned that Jesus quoted it, and all four recorded the cleansing of the temple where Jesus referred to His Father's words (Matthew 21:13; Mark 11:17; Luke 19:46; John 2:17). The fact that the Father's house was to be a house of prayer for all nations was so central to God's plan on earth that Jesus responded to Israel's failure in regard to this with a rare display of godly anger. Evidently, Jesus believed that the people who were a part of God's house should live in accordance with the naming of the house.

This becomes especially relevant to us when we understand that God's house was not in any way limited to the temple in Jerusalem. God's house existed long before the temple or its predecessor, the tabernacle of Moses. And it exists even now and will continue when this age is over and Earth ceases to exist in its current form. It is an eternal house and is forever a place of communion with God.

PRAY and Experience Scripture

First John 5:14–15 says, "And we are confident that he hears us whenever we ask for anything that pleases him."

Pause quietly before the Lord and ask Him to change you, to make you a person who reflects His name. You know this prayer is according to His will, so boldly declare your desire to become more of His "house of prayer." Close with an expression of thanks. "Thank you, Lord, for your Spirit's work in me."

The Bible is filled with references to God's house. As you read through these verses, it becomes very clear that His house has never been limited to a building. The building was an important visual illustration of what it means to draw near to God and to dwell in His presence. Even at the dedication of the first temple, Solomon realized this fact as he prayed, "But will God really dwell on earth with humans? The heavens, even the highest heavens, cannot contain you. How much less this temple I have built!" (2 Chronicles 6:18).

As we begin to understand that the church today is God's house, it is critical that we comprehend what it means to live in or be a house that has been named by God as a house of prayer.

LEARN to Encounter Jesus

You can more easily see yourself as a person and place of prayer when you are empowered by the reality that Jesus is already praying for you.

Pause for a moment and imagine this scene: Jesus is kneeling, quietly bowed in prayer. As you get closer, you can hear Him praying—and He's praying for you! The Savior of the universe is praying for the burdens of your heart and the needs in your life. We know this is true because Romans 8:34 tells us that "He is sitting in the place of honor at God's right hand, pleading for us." What does it do to your heart to know that while you are praying to Jesus, He is praying for you?

When I imagine Jesus is praying just for me, my heart is filled with…

When I remember that Christ sits next to God and talks to Him about my needs, I feel…

Do What He Has Called Us

We often call Pentecost the birthday of the church. Have you considered the correlation between the events of that day and the day when the first temple was dedicated? As Solomon stood before the people and finished praying his great prayer of dedication, there came from heaven what we often call the *shekinah* glory of God. Fire fell from heaven and consumed the sacrifices, and the glory of the presence of the Lord filled the temple. It was clear … God had come to His house!

On the day of Pentecost as the disciples gathered to pray, God once again dedicated His house. Again, fire fell from heaven.

This time the fire didn't come to a building but instead separated and came over the heads of believers. A new temple was dedicated! And you are that temple. God's house is now His people, both when we are gathered in assemblies as well as individually. What hasn't changed is the name. God's house is still a house of prayer for all nations. When it comes right down to it, it's not a matter of debate. The owner of the house gets to name the house. God has clearly, unequivocally named His house a house of prayer. Our job is to figure out what that means and do it!

✚ SHARE with Others in Community

Pause during this final moment to give God thanks. Express your gratitude for how you have freely received God's Spirit.

God, thank You that you have given me the gift of Your Holy Spirit. I am grateful because…

Plan to talk about your experiences of God's presence with another person. When have you sensed His presence, and what difference has that made in your life?

➡ LOVE Others in Community

Just as we have received the blessing of experiencing God's presence, we are called to express His presence to others so they might see Him more clearly and come to know Him (1 John 4:12).

Make plans to demonstrate His presence:

I plan to demonstrate LOVE to those closest to me by…

I plan to LOVE other followers of Jesus by…

I plan to LOVE those who don't know Jesus by…

2

I want to deepen my prayer life and my sensitivity to Your Spirit. I want to become a more faithful disciple of Jesus.

Jesus, reset my prayer life

The gospel of Luke records a surprising interaction. Jesus had gone away to pray in a private place, but when He returned one of the disciples asked, "Lord, teach us to pray…" Isn't it amazing who initiated this conversation? We know Jesus would have considered prayer an important topic for His disciples, but it wasn't Christ who initiated the conversation. Could it be that the Lord wanted the disciples to conclude the importance of prayer on their own? Could it be that He was waiting for them to decide that they wanted to see the power of God demonstrated clearly and consistently in their own lives? Jesus was ready and willing to teach on prayer, but only when His disciples were eager to learn (Luke 11:1–13). So it is with us. Jesus longs to make us a people of prayer.

The prophet Joel reminds us that the stakes are high; our commitment to prayer is of paramount importance.

> Announce a time of fasting; call the people together for a solemn meeting. Bring the leaders and all the people of the land into the Temple of the Lord your God, and cry out to him there. The day of the Lord is near, the day when destruction comes from the Almighty. How terrible that day will be! (Joel 1:14–15)

POWER OF PRAYER AND FASTING

From *Power of Prayer and Fasting*
by Ronnie Floyd

The answer to our spiritual crisis will not be found in the ballot box but in the prayer closet. The answer to our personal and corporate dilemmas will not come through high tech, hyperbole, and hype. It will come through a fresh touch from the Lord, who wants to speak to us, move us, and manifest His mighty presence.

We are in the same condition as God's people during the time of the prophet Joel. The alarm is going off, and we must respond to it. It's time for the church to wake up, just as the priests and the ministers of the Lord in Joel's day were shaken out of their sleep over the sinfulness of Judah. If we are to know God's supernatural power, we, too, must have spirits that are contrite and broken. It broke the priests' hearts that they could not make any offering at all to God. God's judgment had been so mighty that there was nothing left to offer. They wept and wailed before the God of heaven. They humbled themselves through fasting. They demanded national repentance by calling for a solemn assembly to cry out to the Lord. Their tears were expressions of honest grief, and in their pain they interceded for the people of God. They knew this was God's gateway to spiritual power and His gateway to see spiritual breakthrough.

PRAY and Experience Scripture

"Apart from me you can do nothing." (John 15:5)

Pray your own prayer of declaration. Tell God how much you need His help to change your spiritual condition—that apart from Him you can do nothing. As you pray, believe that Jesus is present, available, and sufficient.

Lord, my power and my strength are not sufficient—I need you. I need You to…

How do you read this passage from Joel? Do you see it as another fascinating but perhaps ho-hum history of an ancient people who never seemed to be able to get it together spiritually? Or do you read these verses as a prophetic rendering of where you live today? If we take God's Word at face value, then these words from Joel will do something to challenge our hearts to take action.

They must touch us, break us, and drive us to a new desire to know God. When was the last time we were broken with grief over our own sins and alienation from our heavenly Father? When was the last time we confessed with tears that we were playing church games—just showing up so we could show off—while we knew we were little more than a sordid display of dead men's bones? When did we last intercede on behalf of our bosses, our colleagues at work, or the members of our own families with sorrowful hearts? When was the last time we fasted and prayed over our own spiritual plights, the spiritual conditions of our churches, and the spiritual health of our country? When was the last time we sensed God's calling us to repent of *anything,* especially our separation from the God who made us, loves us, and gave His Son for our eternal souls? When was the last time we were consciously willing to submit to His leadership and willfully to turn from sin when He called us to repent? When was the last time we called for a solemn assembly to cry out for God to forgive us and our brothers and sisters from our sins of racial prejudice, greed, lust, love of material things, and anything else that stands between us and God?

Have we ever been so humbled that we could hardly absorb the presence of God because we knew we were standing on holy ground? In our roles as leaders—and please remember, we are all leaders—have we ever been bold enough, tenacious enough, and spiritually concerned enough to weep at the altar, asking God to bring a mighty spiritual awakening to our lives and to the lives of those around us? If we don't model spiritual humility born from our own deep experiences with God; if we don't model spiritual brokenness; and if we don't model repentance from our self-centeredness and demand for control, we will never see a spiritual revival in our own lives or in the life of our nation.

LEARN to Encounter Jesus

"Who do you say that I am?" (Matthew 16:15)

Pause and meditate on the person of Jesus. Imagine that the resurrected Christ is standing before you. You see His nail-pierced hands, loving face, and glorified body. Imagine that as He stands before you, He gently asks the question, "Who do you say that I am?" Allow the Holy Spirit to move your heart with a response.

Then quietly whisper this prayer: *You are my Lord and I long to know you. Jesus, You are my…*

Now ask Him: *Because You are the Lord of my life, what other priorities, activities, or things do I need to change so that I might better know You?*

Be still and listen for Him to speak. Yield these things to Him. Whatever Jesus asks of you, give it to Him.

For instance: *I know there are things in my life that have become a distraction and are keeping me away from You. I am ready to surrender my…*

When you're ready, make your sincere declaration: *Lord, I want to know You more. I want to love You and serve You!*

As we exercise our spiritual gifts and direct others to this gateway to supernatural power, we will be on our way to personal and national revival. God's people are the keys to this awakening in our time. The church must rise up and lead on!

How do we do this? Joel 2:12–13 says: "Even now—this is the Lord's declaration—'Turn to Me with all your heart, with fasting, weeping, and mourning. Tear your hearts, not just your clothes, and return to the LORD your God.' For He is gracious and compassionate, slow to anger, rich in faithful love, and He relents from sending disaster."

This will be the next great move of God! God's gateway is prayer and fasting. Coming humbly before God is God's gateway to spiritual power and spiritual breakthroughs. The stage is set. Desperation is at an all-time high in our generation. Most churches are missing demonstrations of major spiritual power. Most Christ followers are lacking the manifested presence of God in and through their lives.

God has our attention. A remnant of us must be desperate before Him. We must take action now to pray and fast. When we do, we will ascend the holy hill before God. *May God have mercy upon us and bring on the next great move of God.*

✚ SHARE with Others in Community

After you have sensed God's leading in your life, engage the strength of community: plan to tell another person about how God wants to bring change to your life. Your words might begin like this:

> *I sense that the Lord wants me to change in these ways…*
> *I am committed to praying more consistently about…*
> *I am committed to fasting and prayer as I…*

➜ LOVE Others in Community

Finally, ask God to make these changes and then show you how to more effectively demonstrate His love to others:

> *Change me, Lord, to become more like you. By your Spirit, make me more encouraging, attentive, or compassionate, so that I might better reflect your love. Change me, heavenly Father.*

Floyd, Ronnie, *The Power of Prayer and Fasting* (Nashville, TN: B&H Publishing Group, 2010).

3

I want my life to reflect Your principles, truth, and righteousness. I pray that leaders of the church, government, business, and political arenas demonstrate this same righteousness.

Jesus, reset my prayer life.

If you have accepted Christ's gift of salvation, you have a unique position. You are declared righteous—you are pronounced holy by Christ's saving work. It's important to remember, though, that your position came at great sacrifice. In John 17, Christ reminds us of this price: "And I give myself as a holy sacrifice for them so they can be made holy by your truth" (John 17:19). Jesus prayed for your holiness and your righteousness and then made the ultimate sacrifice: He gave His life so that you can have right standing with God. Our position is secure, but we still need the continued cleansing and character development of the Holy Spirit's work within us. That's the reason Jesus prayed for this process to continue: "Make them holy by your truth" (John 17:17).

Reflect on what God can do when we allow Him to continue to make us holy.

IT'S TIME!

By Doug Stringer

Excerpt republished in October 2014, from the originally
written article in preparation for Houston Prayer Mountain.

The Body of Christ is beginning to awaken. She is preparing herself to reach out as never before. But first, her heart must be stirred and prepared. People are being refreshed and renewed. Strong conviction is drawing hearts back to a right relationship with the Lord. This is only the beginning—a sprinkling of renewal—but we are preparing for the rain.

Most importantly, God is building His character in His church. Hearts that are consecrated to the Lord can contain an outpouring of His Spirit. We must examine our hearts, motives, and actions and then allow the Lord to cleanse us. He must increase and we must decrease. This is the time; this is the hour to prepare for a move of God throughout the land. The late Bro. Leonard Ravenhill said, "God doesn't just answer prayer; He answers desperate prayer."

Genuine passion for God allows no room for mediocrity. Any leaven in our hearts and lives must be purged so that we are consumed with a love for God and His truth. It is what we do behind closed doors where no one else can see us that determines the power of God or lack of it in public.

LEARN to Encounter Jesus

"The student who is fully trained will become like the teacher."
(Luke 6:40)

Imagine that Jesus is standing before you. He is the Master Teacher and you are the student (Matthew 23:10). Reflect on some of the Teacher's attributes: He is the One who is love (1 John 4:8). He is the God of all comfort (2 Corinthians 1:3–4). He is the One who is humble and gentle (Matthew 11:29–30). He is the One who is moved with compassion because of the needs of people (Luke 15:20). He is the One who encourages us in Scripture (Romans 15:4); He bears our burdens and supports us in life's struggles (Galatians 6:2).

Now imagine this: The Teacher invites you to become more like Him, to express His character and His love. He invites you to experience His love so deeply that you become a reflection of Him to those around you.

Pause quietly to pray. Ask His Spirit how you should complete this prayer:

Lord, for me to better reflect your love, I sense it will be important for me to become more _____ with those in my life. Change me Lord; make me like You.

(For example: comforting, gentle, compassionate, encouraging, supportive, truthful, forgiving, respectful, or attentive, etc.)

We must maintain this posture of humility and servanthood if we are to see a genuine move of God. The late Dr. Edwin Louis Cole once said, "You can touch the gold, but don't touch God's glory." Do we desire to bring God the glory? Are we seeking to build His kingdom or our own? Have we surrendered our ministries? Is there any selfish ambition or prejudice? This presents a strong warning to leaders. Do not touch God's glory! God will move by His Spirit. We won't have to work it up or boast of what He is doing. All the glory belongs to the Lord, and we dare not touch it!

We say that we want revival, but do we really understand what that means? As Dr. Michael Brown stated, "Once you pray, 'consume me, Lord,' you can't negotiate with the flames" (From *Holy Laughter to Holy Fire*, p. 74). We must allow the fire of God to consume us so that we become that burnt sacrifice, totally surrendered to the Father's will. That's what our Lord Jesus did, and He requires the same of us—for the cross is the place of total surrender.

PRAY and Experience Scripture

Abraham was described as "the friend of God." And because of this friendship, the Lord paused to share with Abraham all that He was about to do in Sodom and Gomorrah (Genesis 18:17). God paused to reveal His plans to Abraham. This same Lord wants to reveal Himself to you; He wants to share the plans that He has for your life.

Pause now and ask Him:

Lord, I'm listening—how might You want to fulfill your purposes through my life? Speak, Lord—I want to hear You. (1 Samuel 3:8–9)

Listen quietly for the Lord's voice. Give Him time to speak and then thank Him for His friendship.

We are seeing the early signs of a drizzle or a sprinkling.
But soon there will be a downpour of rain. Rain does many things.
It replenishes dry, parched land and it washes away pollutants. And
when the fire of God comes, it will consume and burn out the dross.
It will bring us to our knees. May we have an outpouring of God's
Spirit that washes and burns out the dross, igniting us into a flame
that burns brightly throughout this land. Likewise, may we become
conduits of the river of life, which brings healing wherever it goes.

May there be a worldwide awakening that is deep and wide. If a
thousand years is as one day and one day is as a thousand years as it
says in 2 Peter 3:8, then could it be that we are in the beginning of the
third day since the time of Christ? We live in an exciting time of history.
May we sense a fresh manifested presence of the holiness of God
and a spark of revival through our leaders, our cities, and our nations.

It's your time. May you and I fulfill our destiny for His kingdom and His glory.

✚ SHARE with Others in Community

Pause for a moment and ask God to reveal a specific leader
who needs to experience encouragement, comfort, acceptance, or support—through you! Which of the church, political, business, or community leaders needs to see more of
God shared through you?

*God, please show me one of the leaders of my church or community
who needs more of Your love shared through me.*

Pray for this leader now.

*God, I pray for _____. May he/she reflect Your righ-
teousness. I ask that You empower his/her commitment to Your principles, truth, and standards. I specifically pray for…*

➤ LOVE Others in Community

"No one has ever seen God. But if we love each other, God lives in us, and His love has been brought to full expression through us." (1 John 4:12)

Our genuine love for each other enables the "full expression" of God's love. This means, as others experience God's love through us, they will be able to see Him as He really is. As others receive our acceptance, they will be able to see the God of gracious acceptance (Romans 15:7). Through our demonstration of comfort, others will be able to see the One who is "the Father of compassion and the God of all comfort" (2 Corinthians 1:3 NIV). Through our kindness, others will be able to see the kindness of the Lord (1 Peter 5:10). The experience of love, demonstrated through God's people, can transform how others see God!

Make plans now to share some of God's love with others around you. Begin with those closest to you, then make plans to extend His love to any leader who needs to know Him.

God, I want to share some of Your (acceptance, comfort, kindness etc.) *with…*

I want to love this person so that they will be able to see You more clearly.

4

I want to demonstrate the "fear of the Lord" rather than the approval of people. I want to live a life of credibility and integrity.

Jesus, reset my prayer life.

We rejoice in the miraculous truth that Jesus is busy interceding for us in heaven (Hebrews 7:25). There's a second truth, though, that is just as startling. Jesus is not just praying for us; He's praying for our failures. Think about it: the only One who is qualified to address our behavior is praying for us! Scripture confirms this truth: "And the Holy Spirit helps us in our weakness … for the Spirit pleads for us believers in harmony with God's own will" (Romans 8:26–27). Jesus prays for us while He longs for us to pray to Him!

HE PRAYS FOR US AND LONGS FOR US TO PRAY WITH HIM!

Taken from *The Power of a Praying Church*
by Stormie Omartian and Jack Hayford

God wants each of us to become an intercessor. An intercessor is someone who steps into the gap between God's righteousness and man's failure and, through prayer, brings the merits of the cross to bear upon people and situations.

God wants each one of us to become a member of an army. H*is* army! God is commander-in-chief of this army, and the weapons of choice are prayer, praise, and the Word of God. That's because "though we walk in the flesh, we do not war according to the flesh…" (2 Corinthians 10:3–4). No enemy can stand against these weapons, unless, of course, the enemy convinces us that our weapons are powerless and we stop using them.

God's army is an all-volunteer organization, so we have to enlist. We have to tell God we want to be a part of His army of prayer warriors and ask Him to put us on high alert so we can be mobilized at a moment's notice. The best part about being in God's army is that He goes with us into every battle. He says, "Today you are on the verge of battle with your enemies. Do not let your heart faint, do not be afraid, and do not tremble or be terrified because of them; for the LORD your God is He who goes with you, to fight for you against your enemies, to save you" (Deuteronomy 20:3–4). He tells us to pray, worship Him, and declare His Word, and He will do the rest because "the battle is the LORD's" (1 Samuel 17:47).

PRAY and Experience Scripture

"Fight the good fight for the true faith. Hold tightly to the eternal life to which God has called you…" (1 Timothy 6:12)

In order to live a life that demonstrates a reverence of the Lord and fight the good fight, we must have a firm grip on our calling. Listen as God reminds you of His calling on your life:

Because I have called you to receive the gift of salvation, you now have right standing before Me. I have called you, chosen you, and now you are my holy and beloved people. You are now my treasure. Because of the sacrifice of my Son, I see you as My rich and glorious inheritance. I am delighted to offer you eternal life so that you can share my kingdom and My glory! (Romans 1:6; Romans 8:30; 1 Corinthians 1:2; Galatians 5:13; Ephesians 1:18; 1 Thessalonians 2:12)

Pray now and declare your "tight grip" on these truths.
Because of Your calling and this gift of eternal life, I am most grateful for the truth that…I stand firm and hold tightly to the truth that…

You may be saying to yourself, "How can I make a difference in this world? I'm just one person." But when Samuel prayed on behalf of Israel as the Philistines attacked them, "the LORD thundered with a loud thunder upon the Philistines that day, and so confused them that they were overcome before Israel" (1 Samuel 7:10). Every prayer you pray brings confusion upon the enemy too. If the enemy seems to be winning more and more in our land, it's because we have taken ourselves out of the battle by not praying.

We're not going to change our world by means of political strategies. The world will only be changed in one realm, and that is the spiritual realm. That's why the Bible says we're not wrestling with flesh and blood. Prayer alone will bring a spiritual renewal that will change our world. We need to move as people who recognize our time has come and say, "God, we will take this hour, this moment, and move in prayer with power."

LEARN to Encounter Jesus

"If anyone thirsts, let him come to me and drink. Rivers of living water will brim and spill out of the depths of anyone who believes in me this way" (John 7:38 MSG).

Jesus assured us that if we "drink of His salvation" then everyone who believes in Him will receive the Holy Spirit. If you have received the gift of salvation, then His Spirit lives inside of you. Quietly meditate on this promise of Jesus.

Thank Him for this gift.

Jesus, thank You for the Holy Spirit. I am grateful to have Your living water flowing through me.

First Thessalonians 4:7 tells us that "God has called us to live holy lives." Ask the Lord to wash away anything that might not match the holy life He has called you to; ask Him to bring more integrity to your faith so that you can be a stronger voice for Him.

Jesus, speak to me about any areas of my life where I lack credibility or integrity. Speak to me about any areas where you want to wash me clean. I'm so grateful for the gift of Your Spirit that I want to make sure that my life pleases You. Speak, Lord, I'm listening…

The enemy always tries to keep us distracted with one battle after another in our own personal lives. Battles over our finances, our health, our work, our children, our minds, our emotions, our marriages, our relationships, or whatever front he is attacking us on can be so all-consuming that we don't have time for much else. I know that he wants us so preoccupied with our personal battles that we are always fighting defensively. That way he can wear us out.

Where we go wrong is that we fight from battle to battle and never really enter the war. We think that when we *win* one battle we have *won* the war, and so we stop fighting. And on the other side of that, sometimes when we *lose* a battle we feel we have *lost* the entire war, and so we give up. *What we have to realize is that the war is never over!*

The triumph Jesus won when He said, "It is finished" (John 19:30) broke the power of sin, death, and hell once and for all. But that victory awaits application on earth—and prayer is the warrior's strategy by way of God's assignment. The conflict will not be over until we go to be with the Lord. That's why we must learn to go on the offensive in prayer instead of waiting until something happens and then trying to defend ourselves.

You know how fervently you pray when something goes wrong in your life? Well, God wants us to pray that fervently all the time. He wants us to intercede every day with the same degree of passion we have when we are in the middle of a crisis. The peace that God would like to give us depends upon us doing that.

✚ SHARE with Others in Community

"Use your freedom to serve one another in love." (Galatians 5:13)

Make plans to tell your integrity story. Talk to someone about your commitment to obey the Scriptures and diligent work to lead your life according to His Word. Share how your decision to live out God's Word has actually produced freedom in your life. Your words might begin like this:

I know it sounds crazy, but following God's commands has actually brought more freedom to my life. It's actually been good because...

➤ LOVE Others in Community

Reflect on the relationships that surround you. As an expression of your love for them, spend a few moments in prayer for their integrity and commitment to walk in the fear of the Lord. There is no better way to love than to pray.

God, I pray for _____ (name a specific person). I pray that he/she would feel Your love in relevant ways. Give him/her a fresh sense of Your calling to integrity and holiness. I pray that _____ would live a life that is consumed with pleasing you.

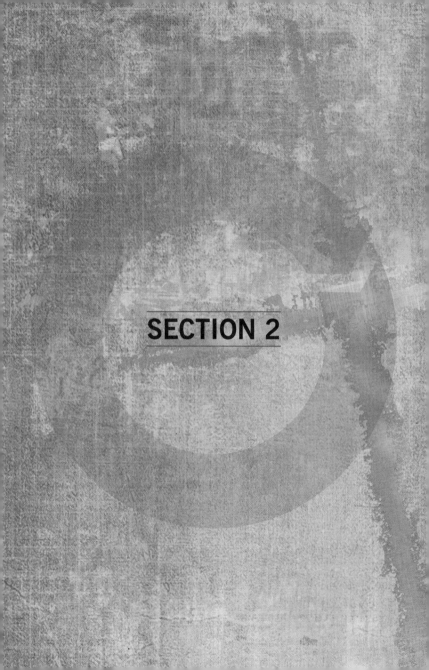

SECTION 2

MY SPIRIT-EMPOWERED FAITH

means that I will love the Word through being a "living epistle" in reverence and awe as His Word becomes real in my life, vocation, and calling.

As I practice this outcome, every aspect of my life will match the truths of His Word, and the Bible will be the explanation for my choices and lifestyle.

Listen as Jesus prays for His Word to be made real in your daily life.

Jesus looked up to heaven and said,
"Father, I have revealed you to the ones you gave me from this world. They were always yours. You gave them to me, and they have kept your word." John 17:6

Now pray with Jesus. Join the prayer meeting that He is already leading on your behalf. *Jesus, please reset my prayer life.*

- I want to live a life of radical generosity. I want to be a person who is committed to compassionate care of others and missional living, and I want to encourage others to do the same.

- I want to be bold in my witness for You. I want to see miracles and dramatic conversions in our day. Make this true of me and more and more of Your people.

- I want to see more expressions of love and unity among all believers, especially among pastors and leaders. I want this to be true of me as well.

- I want to see breakdowns of racial, social, and status barriers in our communities and especially in the household of faith.

5

*I want to live a life of radical generosity.
I want to be a person who is committed
to compassionate care of others and
missional living, and I want to
encourage others to do the same.*

Jesus, reset my prayer life.

Compassion is the word that's used most often to describe the heart of Jesus. The Savior performed amazing, life-giving miracles because of His heart of compassion. He felt deep sorrow for Mary and Martha at the death of their brother; He felt compassion for the man who was deaf; and He felt sorrow for multitudes when they were hungry. When Jesus felt sorrow for the needs of people, He prayed and He acted. Might this be true of us? Let's join Jesus in praying for others and then out of a heart of compassion do something about their needs!

WHEN JESUS PRAYED

From *Ten Key Moments When Jesus Prayed*
by George Wood

People sometimes ask me, "Why should I pray? The Lord knows everything that is going to happen anyway, so do my prayers make a difference?" The fundamental answer to that question is: Jesus told us to pray. But He never asks us to do something He himself did not do. Each of the four gospel writers showed key moments when Jesus prayed.

Jesus prayed at times of deep need in others. The New Testament records three times when tears fell on Jesus' cheeks. The first such occasion was at the grave of Lazarus (John 11:35). The death of their brother, Lazarus, overwhelmed Mary and Martha; Jesus had only deepened their anguish by His delay in coming. They took Jesus to the grave, and He was deeply moved. He ordered the stone removed and then prayed (John 11:41–42). The second time we see Him praying with tears was when, "he approached Jerusalem and saw the city, he wept over it" (Luke 19:41). Finally, the writer of Hebrews said, "During the days of Jesus' life on earth, he offered up prayers and petitions with loud cries and tears to the one who could save him from death" (5:7). He wept fervently for one person, for one city, and for His own submission to the Father's will.

LEARN to Encounter Jesus

Jesus prayed at times out of deep concern for others. Christ prayed because of the sorrow that filled His heart when His friends were hurting. "When Jesus therefore saw her weeping . . . He was deeply moved in spirit and was troubled and . . . Jesus wept" (John 11:33–35 NASB).

Take a moment for your own personal encounter with Jesus. Because He is the same yesterday, today, and forever, He is still sorrowed when we hurt. That means: When your heart is hurting, His heart is hurting. Even when you are disappointed in God or struggle with His response, Jesus hurts for you. Your pain moves His heart with compassion.

Now imagine the face of Jesus as He sees the painful moments of your life. His eyes are filled with tears. The tears are not just for Mary—those tears are for you! Reflect on your own times of loss, disappointment, or sadness, and embrace the truth that the "God of comfort" cares deeply for you (2 Corinthians 1:2–4). Just as Jesus wept for Mary, He weeps for you.

Meditate upon the compassionate face of Jesus. As you picture Christ weeping, allow His care and compassion to touch the hurting places of your heart. Then give Him thanks.

Jesus, when I remember the truth that You hurt when I hurt, I feel...

Thank You for the gift of your compassion. Your compassion gives me hope that...

Jesus prayed in Gethsemane. The place where olives were crushed (the literal meaning of *Gethsemane*) is where Jesus Himself came under great stress. Luke tells us the anguish was so great, His sweat was like drops of blood falling to the ground (Luke 22:41–44). There He prayed three times, "Your will be done" (Matthew 26:36–44). He, who just days earlier raised Lazarus, now declines to extricate himself from a horrendous death. He could easily have risen from prayer, taken the quick walk eastward up the Mount of Olives, and disappeared into the Judean desert. But He stayed … for us. There are times when we are not free to pursue our own comfort and leisure—moments when we must stick by our post of duty. What stabilizes us and gives us fortitude to remain is our life in prayer.

PRAY and Experience Scripture

The story of the Emmaus disciples reminds us of an important position: our position. The travelers heard the "stranger" explain all things concerning the Messiah, and then they invited Jesus to join them for a meal. But the meal began in an unusual way. "When He had reclined at the table with them, He took the bread and blessed it, and breaking it, He began giving it to them" (Luke 24:30 NASB).

Imagine that you have invited Christ into your home, and as you begin the dinner conversation, you notice something unusual. Jesus *invites you* to be seated and takes on the role of gracious host. The Savior offers prayer and begins to serve your meal and your bread to you! This is what it looks like to trust in His presence with us. Our experience of hope, power, and bold compassion can only be realized when we yield our lives to Him, His plan, and His purpose. Jesus, when invited in, takes over!

A significant component of our ability to become a people of compassion will be our commitment to yield to the Holy Spirit as the Comforter. We must assume the position of one who first receives Christ's comfort and then allow Him to empower us to give comfort.

Voice your personal prayer now. Tell God that you are willing to let Him "take over."

God, because You are the God of all compassion and the source of all comfort, I want You to be in charge of my life. I yield to You and how You want to demonstrate compassion through me.

Jesus prayed on the cross. The Gospels, all together, record Jesus speaking seven times from the cross. The first, fourth, and last times were prayers. He began by praying, "'Father, forgive…'" (Luke 23:34). He did not close His fist and shout, "I'll get even with you for this. I'll send you to hell for this." No. He opened His hand, received the nail, and opened His heart to intercede for the very people putting Him to death. He modeled for us that we too must forgive our enemies. His second prayer, the fourth "word" from the cross was, "'My God, my God, why have you forsaken me?'" (Mark 15:34). Yes, at the moment, it appeared God had abandoned Him, but not for long: "He has not despised or disdained the suffering of the afflicted one. … All the families of the nations will bow down before him" (Psalm 22:24–27). We must never give in to the idea that God has abandoned us. There are moments when we feel utter darkness about us, but our end is sure. He will never leave us nor forsake us (Hebrews 13:5). The final word from the cross was His prayer, "'Father, into your hands I commit my spirit'" (Luke 23:46). This is the first prayer every Jewish child learns, much like we teach our children: "Now I lay me down to sleep…" The words are found in Psalm 31:5, except Jesus added one word to the prayer that makes all the difference: "Father." In life and in death, we can trust the Father and commit all that we are to Him.

✚ SHARE with Others in Community

Take the next few moments to allow the Lord to show you the person who needs more of His care and compassion demonstrated through you. Who is going through a struggle and needs you to weep with him or her? Who is facing a life challenge and needs you to sit quietly, listen, and show that you care? Perhaps there is a person in your life who doesn't know Jesus yet but could benefit from a demonstration of His compassion.

God, who needs me to come alongside them and show compassion, just like You have shown compassion to me? Show me that person, Lord. I am listening.

→ LOVE Others in Community

Now that the Lord has spoken to your heart, plan your words of compassion. God tells us in Romans 12:15 to "weep with those who weep." Weeping with someone may literally mean crying with them, but it also means matching their emotion with your emotion. That might sound like this:

I am so sorry that you're going through this. I just want you to know that I care.

It makes me sad to know that . . . Please know that I am praying for you.

I feel a lot of compassion for you right now. I am here for you and ready to listen.

Out of gratitude go and share some of the compassion that you have received from Jesus.

6

I want to be bold in my witness for You.
I want to see miracles and dramatic
conversions in our day.
Make this true of me and
more and more of your people.

Jesus, reset my prayer life.

Jesus was eager to spend His final moments before the cross with the disciples. Christ's words reassured them of His desire: "With fervent desire I have desired to eat this Passover with you before I suffer" (Luke 22:15 NKJV). This special moment was meaningful to the Savior, to his disciples, and ultimately for us, His followers. Christ's vulnerability in the upper room revealed the topics that were most dear to Him. Jesus' desire was for His followers to experience the same power and boldness that He did. Remember Christ's prayer: "As You sent Me into the world, I also have sent them into the world" (John 17:17 NKJV). Jesus was sent to earth with power and boldness. He was sent into the world with dramatic conversions and miracles. If He prayed for us to experience the same, what went wrong?

PRAY LIKE IT MATTERS

From *Pray Like It Matters*
by Steve Gaines

A growing number of Christians today are aware that something must be wrong. They know there has to be "more" to the Christian life than what they have experienced. "More" is found through the discipline of prayer. When we begin to pray like Jesus and His early followers, then we will witness the power they experienced.

When I read the book of Acts, I am embarrassed. Why does our brand of Christianity look so insipid compared to the believers of the first century? Where has the power gone? Has God changed, or have we? We've all heard the cop-out, "The book of Acts represents a different dispensation." What a sad, self-serving attempt to excuse our current state of spiritual impotence!

When we read Acts, we should yearn to experience a return to their brand of Christianity. Yet, instead of copying them, we seem content with copying other modern churches that are "growing." But *why copy a copy, when you can copy the original (the book of Acts)?* In Acts, God was saving people every day. Communities were transformed. People were healed. Demons were cast out. Miracles were commonplace. Churches sprouted up across the Roman Empire. Persecution was faced and overcome. What made them so different?

Our lack of spiritual power in Christianity today is not due to the sermons we preach or the songs we sing. Rather, *it is due to our lack of prayer.* We do not pray like it matters. Jesus and His earliest followers prayed like it was important. We pray like it is inconvenient or inconsequential. Prayer was their priority. It is our postscript. We plan more than we pray. The Christians of the early church prayed more than they planned. We gather to minister to one another. They gathered to minister to the Lord in prayer and fasting. Our focus is earthly, horizontal. Theirs was heavenly, vertical.

LEARN to Encounter Jesus

Many of us know what it means to minister *for* the Lord, but how many of us know how to minister *to* the Lord? Acts 13:2 tells us that the first disciples ministered "*to* the Lord" (NKJV). What does it mean to minister to Jesus? It means to serve Him, to love Him, to have a vertical focus of priority in relationship with Him. What a different motive for prayer. It's not just something that we should *do*, it's a part of how we love the Lord!

Pause and allow the Holy Spirit to bring an image of Jesus to your mind and heart. Imagine the scene: Jesus is sitting at the home of His friends, Mary and Martha. He has just experienced rejection in the Samaritan village but has rejoiced over the good reports from the seventy who were sent out (Luke 9:51–56; Luke 10:1–22). Imagine how Mary senses the Savior's sadness about Jerusalem, as well as His celebration for those seventy disciples. Notice Mary. Where is she? She sits at Jesus' feet—listening to Him. Mary is loving Jesus, ministering *to* Him. We're shocked to hear Martha's interruption, but also startled by Christ's clear words of affirmation: "Mary has chosen what is better" (Luke 10:42 NIV).

Now imagine that you have the same opportunity to minister to Jesus. In truth, you do! You have this same opportunity to love Him, serve Him, and minister to Him in prayer!

He is waiting. He has taken a seat in your home. Sit quietly with a reverent heart. Do not speak at first; just listen. The Savior longs to share His heart. Wait before Him. Listen for His words of pleasure: "You have chosen well."

Now allow the Spirit within you to commune with the Savior. Talk to Him in prayer, but make these moments a two-way conversation. Listen to Him. Wait for His response. Then tell Him the concerns of your heart.

✚ SHARE with Others in Community

Spend a few moments in quiet reflection. Ask the Lord to show you a person who could benefit from hearing what God is doing in your life. Who might need to hear about the truth that prayer is one of the best ways to minister to Jesus? Your story might begin with these words:

Jesus is doing some amazing things in my life…
I'd love to share how prayer has changed me…

Every prayer we pray is significant. Through our prayers, God changes things. One life dedicated to prayer can do more good than any life dedicated to other so-called "noble," worldly causes. An individual follower of Jesus who is committed to prayer is a fountain of life in a world of death. Likewise, the local church that becomes a house of prayer will be a spiritual powerhouse from which God's mighty miracles will flow exponentially. Prayer is what modern Christians and churches are missing—*frequent, fervent, faithful prayer*!

THE POWER OF PRAYING FERVENTLY

Churches today should resemble the churches mentioned in the book of Acts. When we read Acts and then analyze our twenty-first-century churches, we are forced to ask, "Where is the power of God?" Indeed, why do we see so few people being saved? Why aren't more people healed physically? Why don't we experience demons being cast out of people? Why aren't entire cities coming to Christ as they burn their pagan paraphernalia like the new Christians did in the city of Ephesus (Acts 19)? Why aren't modern-day Christians "turning their world upside down" (Acts 17:6) with the gospel?

Read these wonderful words: "Peter was in prison, but prayer for him was being made fervently by the church to God" (Acts 12:5). Appreciate the contrast intended by the writer: "Peter was in prison, *but prayer…*" (emphasis mine). The prayers prayed for Peter were far from being casual or routine. Instead, they were urgent, desperate, and fervent prayers. The Greek word translated "fervently" in Acts 12:5 is *ektenos*. It means to pray "eagerly; fervently; constantly." Fervent prayers rise from a boiling, passionate heart that pleads with God and must have an answer! It's the kind of prayer Jacob offered when he wrestled with the Angel of the Lord. "I will not let you go unless you bless me" (Genesis 32:26). God loves it when His children pray with such fervency!

The fact is, Jesus prayed with fervency. When He was in the garden of Gethsemane, just before He was arrested, Luke tells us, "And being in agony He was praying very fervently; and His sweat became like drops of blood, falling down upon the ground" (Luke 22:44). Jesus poured out His heart in passionate, fervent prayer to His Father, just like His followers did later in Acts 12 on behalf of Peter. The Father answered Jesus, and He also answered those who interceded for Peter. What could happen if we prayed fervently?

🗨 PRAY and Experience Scripture

What about you? What concern of your life could benefit from your fervent prayer? What issue needs your eager and constant prayer?

James 5:16 tells us that "the effective, fervent prayer of a righteous man avails much" (NKJV). Prayer accomplishes things! So here is your chance to pray earnestly. Minister to Jesus in these next moments; bring to Him the deepest concerns of your heart. Ask Jesus for a miracle or a dramatic conversion and trust Him to accomplish it.

Jesus, the issue that concerns my heart right now is…
I need to sit at Your feet because…
Speak to me about this. I am listening.

➡ LOVE Others in Community

Spend the next few moments asking the Lord to show you the person who could benefit from your prayer. Who needs your earnest prayer on their behalf? Ask God to reveal this person and then listen.

God, I sense that You want me to pray more earnestly for _____ (name a person), because…

$\overline{7}$

I want to see more expressions of love and unity among all believers, especially among pastors and leaders. I want this to be true of me as well.

Jesus, reset my prayer life.

Unity: Scripture tells us it's important. Paul reminds us that unity is evidence of our maturity and of a life lived out in a manner worthy of our calling (Ephesians 4:1–4, 13). We also see the importance of unity because it defines the Trinity. The Father, Son, and Holy Spirit operate in perfect harmony and oneness. Unity, it seems, is a divine commodity. Jesus' prayer in John 17 is confirmation: "May they experience such perfect unity that the world will know that you sent me and that you love them as much as you love me" (John 17:23). Jesus cares about unity because when there is oneness among God's people, the world takes notice and is drawn to Him!

THE PRAYER LIFE OF JESUS CHRIST

Taken from *The Praying Church Handbook*, Volume II
by Dr. Mark Williams

Among the many qualities, the single, most impressive quality that characterized the life of Jesus, leaving a definite imprint on the lives of His disciples, was the fact that Jesus was a man of prayer. True enough, Jesus Christ was the Messiah. True enough, Jesus Christ was God. True enough, Jesus Christ was meek and lowly. True enough, Jesus Christ was a powerful teacher. True enough, Jesus Christ could turn water into wine, perform miracles by the roadside, heal the multitudes without medicine, cleanse the lepers, and even raise the dead. But never once do you read the disciples saying, "Lord, teach us to preach." Never once do you find them saying, "Lord, teach us to perform miracles." Never once do you see the disciples huddled around Jesus, saying, "Lord, teach us to raise the dead." No. But in Luke 11:1, after Jesus had finished praying, one of His disciples came to Him and said, "Lord, teach us to pray."

Jesus was a man of prayer, and He taught much about the dynamics of prayer. In Matthew 5:44, Jesus said we are to pray for those who despitefully use and persecute us. In Matthew 6:5–9, Jesus said we are to pray without hypocrisy. In Matthew 9:38, we are told to pray to the Lord of the harvest to send forth laborers into His harvest. In Matthew 26:41, He said we are to "watch and pray" so that we don't enter into temptation. In Mark 11:25, Jesus said when we stand to pray, forgive, if we have anything against another person, so that He will hear our prayer and forgive us. And in Mark 11:24, "Therefore I say to you, whatever things you ask when you pray, believe that you receive them, and you will have them" (NKJV). Jesus clearly communicated the power of prayer!

🗨 PRAY and Experience Scripture

"Behold, I am the servant of the Lord; let it be to me according to your word." (Luke 1:38 ESV)

In this brief moment of prayer, Mary voiced complete surrender to God. Even before she knew what the future held, Mary yielded. She didn't yet know what was to be required of her; she didn't know what would be asked of her, but Mary declared her yieldedness to God. Would you pray this same prayer?

God, I say yes to whatever you have for my future. I know unity among Your people is important to You because it draws others to You. So whatever You have in store for me and the unity you want me to display, I am yielded. Without knowing all that You might ask of me, I yield to Your will.

Jesus not only taught about prayer, Jesus prayed. In Matthew 14:23, "And when He had sent the multitudes away, He went up into a mountain apart to pray: and when the evening was come, He was there alone." In Mark 1:35, "And in the morning, rising up a great while before day, He went out, and departed into a solitary place, and there prayed." In John 17, we read that great, high priestly prayer just before Christ's agony, climaxing in verses 20 and 21: "Neither pray I for these alone, but for them also which shall believe on me through their word, that they all may be one; as thou, Father, art in me, and I in thee, that they also may be one in us: that the world may believe that thou hast sent me."

PRAY and Experience Scripture

Christ's prayer reminds us that we are each called to unity and to be a people who care. In truth, a caring community is to be one of the distinctive characteristics of Jesus-followers. First Corinthians 12:25 clearly spells out the contrast: "So that there may be no division in the body, but that the members may have the same care for one another" (NASB).

Pause quietly and consider: Who could benefit from receiving care from you? Who might need your demonstration of care as a way to bring unity and oneness? Ask God to reveal this person and how you might share some of His love for this person.

Lord, who could benefit from my care? Who needs more of Your love, care, and kindness demonstrated through me? Show me this person and what they might need.

Now listen. Thank Him that you hear His voice, and plan to express this care within the next few days. Yield to Him and become a "living letter" of unity and care.

Jesus' prayers are answered! On the cross, Jesus prayed, "Father, forgive them, for they know not what they do." After the resurrection, when Jesus ascended back to heaven, He took His place by the right hand of the Father and prayed. He promised in John 14:16, "And I will pray the Father, and He shall give you another Comforter, that He may abide with you forever." And that prayer was answered on the day of Pentecost!

Right now, Jesus is praying for you. There is one God and one mediator between God and man: the Man, Christ Jesus. Hebrews 7:25 says, "He ever lives to make intercession for us!"

For we have not a high priest which cannot be touched with the feeling of our infirmities; but was in all points tempted like as we are, yet without sin. Let us therefore come boldly unto the throne of grace, that we may obtain mercy, and find grace to help in time of need. (Hebrew 4:15–16)

Is it any wonder, after watching Jesus pray, seeing the fervency of His prayer, the frequency of His prayer, the power of His prayer, and the intimate relationship with which He communicated with the Father, that the disciples came to Jesus and said, "Lord, teach us to pray"?

 LEARN to Encounter Jesus

What does it do to your heart to know that the Savior is praying for you? He sits at the right hand of the Father and talks to God on your behalf. How does that make you feel toward Jesus? Tell Him now.

Jesus, when I imagine that You are in heaven right now, praying for me, I feel...

I am thankful to have a mediator like You, who...

What's our response? The disciples' request reveals that there is a right way and a wrong way to pray. So, Lord, teach us how to pray. But more than **how** to pray, teach us to pray. Teach us to pray instead of worry. Teach us to pray instead of fear. Teach us to pray instead of gossip. Teach us to pray instead of accuse. Teach us to pray instead of slander. Teach us to pray instead of retaliate in anger. Teach us to pray instead of harboring bitterness.

Teach us to pray instead of devising our own schemes. More than perform miracles, more than preach effectively, more than teach, more than possess the favor of men, **Lord, teach us to pray**!

SHARE with Others in Community

Reflect on the relationships you have with other members of the body of Christ. Do you only have relationships with believers who are like you? Ask the Lord to reveal any areas of needed growth.

Lord, show me any areas where I could take steps to increase the unity among God's people.

Next, pray specifically for the pastors and leaders of your church. Join Jesus in praying that they, too, would be unified with other believers so that the world might be drawn to Him.

God, I pray for my pastors and leaders. May they sense the urgency of expressing unity. Empower them to grow in their love for one another.

Finally, tell another person how Jesus is resetting your commitment to unity.

LOVE Others in Community

As a practical demonstration of unity, send a note to a pastor, teacher, church leader, parent, or mentor, expressing gratitude for how this person has blessed you.

Plan your words of appreciation here:

I am especially grateful for _____ (name a specific person) *because he/she has* (helped me, inspired me, encouraged me, challenged me, cared for me, supported me). *I am thankful specifically for…*

8

I want to see breakdowns of racial, social, and status barriers in our communities and especially in the household of faith.

Jesus, reset my prayer life.

In praying for future believers, Jesus relayed this hope in John 17:20: "I do not pray for these alone, but also for those who will believe in Me through their word; that they all may be one, as You, Father, are in Me, and I in You; that they also may be one in us, that the world may believe that You sent Me." Given the ongoing state of racial mistrust in America, the caring testimony of the church is a must in order for us to experience the unity that Christ longs for. It certainly won't be easy, but unity is required for lasting change. It's not just about getting along; it's about getting it right. Only great diversity, in unison, can bring us to our better selves.

SEVEN BRIDGES OF RECONCILIATION
From the article,
"The Reconciled Church: Seven Bridges of Reconciliation"
featuring Bishop Harry Jackson with Raphael Green

The atmosphere in our culture has reached a critical, if not powder-keg, stage. Violent protests have become symbolic of the racial divide in America and clear, unabashed examples of the need for racial reconciliation and criminal justice reform.

It is the church—God's people—that must spearhead the movement and lead the way in racial reconciliation, societal reform, and changes in the current criminal justice system. It is only through a unified church and adherence to Jesus' prayer in John 17 that we will heal the racial divide in this country and prompt justice system officials to bring about the much-needed change in the way they handle volatile situations.

The greatest source of influence over this nation should be the church. We've tried to make government another pharaoh—our source of provision and hope. Consequently, we've been kept in bondage by a system we have erroneously put our trust in. We need to get an answer to Jesus' prayer, and immediately. Father God is looking at us right now. He sees His family, the church. And God wants that family to love their Father so much that they love each other.

LEARN to Encounter Jesus

Take the next few moments to reflect on Christ's final moments with His disciples. Revisit the emotions that must have filled the upper room. Jesus knows He is only hours from the cross; His time with the disciples is short. He tenderly washes the disciples' feet in an ultimate gesture of humility and service. He reassures them of the kingdom that awaits them. He reassures them of the Comforter who will come. And then out of this heart of love, Jesus makes a bold declaration. Jesus is about to die a horrible death, so the words He says must be important. His words also have importance because Christ gives a command, and only God gives commandments! "So now I am giving you a new commandment: Love each other. Just as I have loved you, you should love each other. Your love for one another will prove to the world that you are my disciples" (John 13:34).

Christ gives *us* this same command. The one who humbly sacrificed Himself for you and died a horrific death for you gives a command. Jesus has a heavenly kingdom that awaits you; He gives the Holy Spirit that's ever present. And now Christ, Himself, gives a command: Love others like I love you.

Talk to Jesus. Tell Him about your willingness to love others just as He has loved you. Without regard for race or status, tell Jesus that you are willing to yield to His command.

Jesus, I know that You love me with extravagant love. I am willing to obey your command and share this love with others so that the world will know You.

When the church employs seven bridges of reconciliation, we can bring about transformation within our communities. These seven bridges are described below. For our communities to experience change:

We need gatherings of Christian, interdenominational, and multiethnic believers to lift up specific prayer points. In order for reconciliation to occur, prayer must be perpetually offered to God requesting wisdom and divine aid for the multigenerational fulfillment of the Great Commandment (John 17:1–26) and the Great Commission (Matthew 28:18–20). We also need periodic voluntary engagement in transparent, honest, frank, civil, and godly dialogue; and the implementation of plans of action to confront, overcome, and resolve destructive views, values, convictions, preferences, and practices (like racism, sexism, ageism, etc.) that divide the Lord's church, misrepresent Jesus Christ, defame God's creation, and hinder the fulfillment of the Great Commandment and the Great Commission.

We need the church's involvement in order to foster academic skills in the lives of our young people. God's people must work together to increase access to early educational programs prior to kindergarten for children. Churches can play a major role in offering academic and character-building enrichment programs to students in middle and high school.

We need to address citizen and law enforcement rights and issues while engaging in civic responsibilities. The church can play a vital role in helping to emphasize and educate in Christian citizenship training. Wise community leaders will review best practices for dealing with citizen and law enforcement rights and issues that threaten to denigrate, deteriorate, debilitate, or devastate the highest quality of life for urban residents.

We need strategic efforts identified in order to serve under-resourced residents in financially depressed zones of our urban community. Compassionate outreach efforts are needed to serve the poverty-stricken residents living in economically devastated areas of our communities. Models must include services such as counsel and representation for legal issues, financial assistance, housing, education, healthcare programs, and employment training.

PRAY and Experience Scripture

"'I tell you the truth, when you refused to help the least of these my brothers and sisters, you were refusing to help me.'" (Matthew 25:45)

Read the passage above carefully. Allow Christ's words to penetrate your heart. When we refuse to help the "least of these" in our communities, it's as if we are refusing to help our Savior. Pause for a moment and ask the Lord to reveal any times when perhaps you have seen the needs of the poor, the less educated, or people of a different economic status or race—and yet not been willing to help. Ask His Spirit to show you any needed areas of growth.

Jesus, show me any times that I passed by the needs of others and was unwilling to help. I know that I hurt You at those times, and my heart is grieved. Change me.

We must nurture the divine sanctity of life, identity, purpose, and destiny through programs for marriages and families. The church can help facilitate transformation by providing services that will help to introduce, rebuild, or enhance the sanctity of life, the discovery of personal and relational identity, and the relevance of healthy marriages and families. Church leaders can help citizens navigate the fulfillment of this vision through seminars, counseling, youth athletic programs, pro-life services, and biblical marriage and family training. Mentoring and fatherhood initiatives will be a key component of family development.

We need strategic involvement with the criminal justice system and a plan for reform. The need for minority engagement with the criminal justice system is at the core of our current tensions. Transformation would include training for prison evangelism workers and regional partnerships for prison aftercare and job creation. Outreach to the incarcerated is a strategic opportunity to bring transformation and reconciliation. The church is needed to reach those behind bars by sharing the gospel of Jesus Christ. This aspect of service is a specific way that the church can reach out to love the least, last, and the lost.

We need to equip churches in how to encourage ethical capitalism. In addition to personal financial training, credit repair, and benevolence, many other dimensions of economic equipping can be launched within churches. Investment training, schools of business, and specific entrepreneurial training plans can be developed, providing hope to even the poorest communities.

As the church models unity—as God's people address the racial divide in our own house—new things can happen. We will see more clearly that we have not just a race problem, but a class problem, a poverty problem, and a spiritual problem. Church, government, business, together we stand—together we can revitalize education, economic development, and justice—or divided we fall.

SHARE with Others in Community

Plan a conversation with another person. Tell them how Jesus has reset your priorities. Tell them how Jesus has loved you and now you are committed to loving others, regardless of race or status.

LOVE Others in Community

Think carefully about how you might give to "the least of these" in your community. And remember, as you give, you are giving to Jesus! Make an intentional plan for how you will demonstrate Christ's love to those who are of a different economic or educational status.

I am committed to helping Jesus by serving others as I...

SECTION 3

MY SPIRIT-EMPOWERED FAITH

will mean that I love people by ministering Christ's life and love to my nearest ones at home and with family, as well as faithful engagement in His body, the church.

As I practice this outcome, I will live like Jesus around those who are closest to me, with other Jesus-followers, and with those He cares most about.

Listen as Jesus prays for your relationships and demonstrations of love so that others will know Him.

> **Jesus looked up to heaven and said,**
> *"Father, I am in them and you are in me.*
> *May they experience such perfect unity that the*
> *world will know that you sent me and that you*
> *love them as much as you love me."* John 17:23

Now pray with Jesus. Join the prayer meeting that He is already leading on your behalf. *Jesus, please reset my prayer life.*

- Renew my commitment to my own marriage. Help me live out a covenant relationship with my spouse. Help us all see a decrease in divorce and a renewed celebration of marriage as God intended.

- I want to come alongside pastors and church leaders and lift them up in prayer. Make their lives characterized by joy, loving relationships, and a spiritual passion that ignites the faith of others. As I love God's people, make these characteristics true of me and my life.

- I want to see the gospel address abortion and increase our deliberate care for children, especially through adoption and foster care. Let the well-being of children be among our highest priorities.

- I want to see more examples of righteous relationships around me. I want my relationships to be pleasing to You most of all!

9

Renew my commitment to my own marriage. Help me live out a covenant relationship with my spouse. Help us all see a decrease in divorce and a renewed celebration of marriage as God intended.

Jesus, reset my prayer life.

It is intriguing that the epic saga of the almighty Creator of the universe's intimate disclosure of Himself to His creation—the Bible—begins and ends with marriage. From the first chapter of Genesis (1:27) to the last chapter of Revelation (22:17), God's love story unfolds within the context of marriage.

Genesis reminds us of God's heart for unity in marriage. Revelation reminds us of His eternal commitment to His bride. John 17 reminds us that unity, the holy union of relationships, is a reflection of His glory. "The glory which You gave Me I have given them, that they may be one just as We are one: I in them, and You in Me…" (John 17:22 NKJV).

Jesus cares about marriage because it reflects a holy union of relationships. Let's join Jesus in prayer for marriage because love, the deepest yearning and need of the human heart, mirrors the magnificent expression and reflection of the Creator's heart!

MAKING MAGNIFICENT MARRIAGES

From *Making Magnificent Marriages*
by Dr. Jared Pingleton

Everyone longs to love and be loved. It has been said that love is the universal human language; it is the expression of caring for someone beyond ourselves. Unlike anything else, the rosy and romantic topic of love has inspired poets, playwrights, and philosophers down through the ages as they have extolled its virtues and vicissitudes.

Clearly, the almighty Sovereign God—who is love personified (1 John 4:7–12)—designed us in love, for love, to love (Luke 10:27; 1 Peter 1:22; 1 John 4:16–21) out of His everlasting love for us (Jeremiah 31:3). As Christ followers, love is to be the definition of our identity, the declaration of our intentions, and the demonstration of our integrity (John 13:34–35, 15:10–12). It's actually pretty easy to love someone who is lovable, lovely, and loving. As a matter of fact, that just seems to be reflexive human nature. But Jesus turned this natural tendency of human nature upside down when He asked rhetorically, "If you love those who love you, what reward will you get? Are not even the tax collectors doing that?" (Matthew 5:46). Obviously, if even IRS agents can love those who love them, Jesus doesn't sound very impressed!

PRAY and Experience Scripture

"To the praise of the glory of His grace..." (Ephesians 1:6 NASB)

Pause to reflect upon your personal experience of God's love and grace. When have you received His love? Be still and ask His Spirit to stir up memories of times when you were loved. Times when He graciously and lovingly...

- provided for you.
- accepted you in the midst of a failure.
- healed your physical or emotional pain.
- restored a broken relationship.

Now, voice your prayer:

God, I give thanks and praise to You for the love You gave me when...

What's harder—and therefore requires an unconditional covenant—is to care for and love someone who isn't always lovable, lovely, and loving. It is at this level of depth that actually and actively loving one's marriage partner becomes realistic instead of romantic.

God loves us because of His *lovingness*, not because of our *lovability*. God is proactive, not reactive. One of the most impressive things about Jesus' character is that He never immaturely reacted to anyone or any situation. Unlike us, He was entirely and exclusively self-controlled and, therefore, always and only proactive (John 10:17). God loves us because of who and how He is, not because of who or how *we* are. No matter what we do or don't do, Jesus cannot love us any more—or any less—than He does right now! It's really not about us; our being loved by God is all about Him. In the same way, in our marriages **true love is more about the character of the lover than the characteristics of the beloved!**

This concept is both radical and revolutionary. It is radical because it is counter to and in conflict with everything that our culture teaches us about love, and it contradicts the natural reflexes of our flesh. It is revolutionary because it has the potential and the power to permanently transform marriages like possibly nothing else can.

As Stephen and Alex Kendrick explain in their fantastic instruction manual about how to proactively love someone who is not necessarily being loving or lovable, "The truth is this: love is not determined by the one *being* loved but rather by the one *choosing* to love" (*The Love Dare*, 2008, p. 46).

The truth is that mature love is not based on feelings, fancy, or fickleness. Warm and fuzzy loving feelings are the result, not the cause of love. Mature "agape" love is both self-generated and other-focused. We are to love our spouse no matter what, and we are to be committed to doing what is best for their welfare no matter what it costs us. Genuine love always has an altruistic attitude and agenda.

LEARN to Encounter Jesus

God does not want us to take the gifts that He has given for granted. He reminds us clearly: *"not to receive the grace of God in vain."* (2 Corinthians 6:1 ESV). Here's what this means for marriage.

- Husbands, you have been gifted with a wife (Proverbs 18:22).
- Wives, can you receive your husbands as gifts from above (James 1:17)?

Take a few moments to pray in the confident faith of 1 John 5:14–15. Pray a prayer that you can be certain is according to God's will. Pray with sincerity:

Lord, I receive my wife/my husband as a gift from You. I recommit myself to joining You in treating my partner as a treasured gift. May You continue to build our home according to Your ways.

When we expect another person to love us and make us happy, we are bound to be disappointed eventually. By expecting our spouse to make us happy, we subconsciously idolize them in place of God. As with so many other things, we are unintentionally and unwittingly tempted to worship and adore the creation instead of the Creator. We confuse the vehicle (marriage) with the destination (God's will for our lives).

God meant for us to find Him through marriage—not in marriage! No matter how winsome and wonderful a marriage partner may be, no spouse is worthy of worship all day every day. The inevitable hurts and heartaches of marriage should drive us to divinity—not to divorce. Our spouse is not our ultimate source; God is.

→ LOVE Others in Community

Imagine that Jesus is standing before you; His eyes are full of compassion and His heart is full of love. If you listen closely, you hear Him say, "Come to me, all of you who are weary and carry heavy burdens, and I will give you rest. Take my yoke upon you. Let me teach you, because I am humble and gentle at heart, and you will find rest for your souls" (Matthew 11:28–29).

You might imagine Jesus with flowing robes and sandals. You might see Christ with bearded face and nail-pierced hands. But as you look closer, you notice that Jesus is standing in a yoke. One side of the yoke is around Him, while the other is empty. Jesus extends His invitation to you: "Take my yoke upon you, my beloved. This simple tool was used long ago, but its symbolism applies today. A yoke was used on a farm for more experienced animals to teach the young ones. So, learn from me. Let me teach you how to love your spouse well." This is your invitation to join Him, to *partner with the One who is love in order to give His love to others.*

Listen as you hear Christ speak to you:

- "I consistently love those around you, but I often do so alone—would you come join me?"
- (To husbands) "I regularly support and comfort your wife, but I often do it without you—would you come and join me?"

- (To wives) "I frequently encourage and affirm your husband, but I often do it without you—would you come and join me?"
- "I consistently take initiative to love the people in your life, but I often do so without you—let me teach you what I know."

Now meditate on your response to Jesus' invitation. In your own mind and heart, picture yourself rising to join Christ in the yoke. Imagine yourself standing alongside the One who is love.

Talk to Jesus about your willingness to join Him in the yoke. Thank Him that He will be your teacher and guide.

✚ SHARE with Others in Community

Plan a time to share about this moment with your spouse. Tell your husband or wife about your commitment to join Jesus in loving well. Your words might begin with these:

I've spent some time with Jesus in prayer. He invited me to join Him in loving you well.

Because I love you, I've asked Jesus to show me how to...

10

I want to come alongside pastors and church leaders and lift them up in prayer. Make their lives characterized by joy, loving relationships, and a spiritual passion that ignites the faith of others. As I love God's people, make these characteristics true of me and my life.

Jesus, reset my prayer life.

One of the special celebrations of Christ's heart was His provision of the Word. He even reaffirmed this certainty in His prayer to the Father, "I told them many things while I was with them in this world so they would be filled with my joy. I have given them your word" (John 17:13–14). With Jesus' great gift comes great accountability: Christ's followers (and particularly church leaders) are called to be good stewards of God's Word. The apostle Paul reminds us, "Be diligent to present yourself approved to God as a workman who does not need to be ashamed, accurately handling the Word of truth" (2 Timothy 2:15 NASB). Accurately handling the Word also includes our ability to live it out. So how's your diligence? How are you doing at living out God's Word with reverence and accuracy?

DILIGENCE IN MINISTRY

From blogposts by Dr. Michael Lewis and Dr. Mark Dance
Mark Dance: @markdance
Michael Lewis: mlewis@namb.net

DILIGENCE MAY MEAN A BREAKUP

It is difficult to be diligent about living God's Word when we expose ourselves to so much useless media. Think about the primary cultural influences on our mind: cable television, radio, Facebook, Twitter, and Instagram, just for starters! The sheer volume of this media distracts and drains our brains—as does much of its content.

So what are we going to do about it? Well, perhaps we should just break up with cable TV and subscription radio. Or maybe it's time to do a painful purge of friends and followers on Facebook, Twitter, and Instagram? We're all looking for greater influence in this world, but at the same time isn't there often too much noise in it? For many of us, we may need more than a temporary media fast; we may need an intentional decision followed by deliberate recalibration. Let's start this recalibration in our thought life.

DILIGENCE IN OUR THOUGHTS

"Be transformed by the renewing of your mind." (Romans 12:2)

Our minds are working all the time. Donna Seal, a licensed therapist, has identified three categories for our thoughts.

1. Some thoughts are TRUTHFUL

We can love God with all our minds by consistently uploading the truth of God's Word. We can also intentionally replace the lies of the world, flesh, and devil with His truth. Approximately 50,000 thoughts go through our heads a day, and not all of them are true.

2. Some thoughts are HELPFUL

Helpful thoughts are both good and true. Loving God with all of our minds is good biblical theology, not merely secular psychology. In Philippians 4:8, we are reminded that God will guard the minds of those who dwell/think on whatever is honorable, just, pure, lovely, commendable, or morally excellent.

3. Some thoughts are HOPEFUL

Hopeful thinking is not the same as wishful thinking. Hopeful thoughts are true, but also hard. For instance, "I'm not doing okay (hard truth), *but* I can get better with God's help (helpful truth)." Some of our thoughts are true but just plain hard to take, especially when the truth stings.

Under the lordship of Christ, our thoughts can be a source of truth, joy, and strength.

PRAY and Experience Scripture

"Fix your thoughts on what is true, and honorable, and right, and pure, and lovely, and admirable. Think about things that are excellent and worthy of praise ... Then the God of peace will be with you." (Philippians 4:8–9)

Spend the next few moments reflecting on the parts of your life that cause anxiety, worry, stress, or heartache. Imagine those circumstances and the thoughts that go with them as fiery arrows, intent on causing harm. Talk to the God of peace about these things, and then ask Him to replace those thoughts with His.

Jesus, I know my thoughts are not always on things that are excellent, especially when I think about…

Holy Spirit, as the guard of my mind and my heart, would you replace these unhealthy thoughts with Yours? Instead of those fiery arrows, what true, lovely, right, pure, and honorable thoughts do you want me to have? Tell me, Lord. I'm listening…

DILIGENCE IN OUR SERVICE

The only mind-set of ministry that God blesses is one of humble service for others; this humble mind-set is to be prayerfully pursued as we serve where the Lord has appointed us. One theme of Philippians 2 is "mind-set for ministry," and this theme causes us to ask introspectively, "What is my mind-set for ministry?" The apostle Paul exhorts us:

"Do nothing from selfishness or empty conceit, but with *humility of mind* regard one another as more important than yourselves. Do not merely look out for *your own personal interest*, but also for *the interest of others*. Have *this attitude* in yourselves which was also in Christ Jesus…" (Philippians 2:3–5, emphasis added).

Paul, speaking of Timothy, again mentions how rare a humble mind-set is in ministry as he commends Timothy: "For I have no one else of kindred spirit who will genuinely be concerned for your welfare. For they all *seek after their own interest*, not those of Christ Jesus" (Philippians 2:20–21, emphasis added).

What is our mind-set of ministry? Are we serving for selfish promotion and image, *or* are we serving with the humble mind-set of Christ for the benefit and well-being of others? This question will determine the motivation of every sermon that's prepared, every hospital or nursing home visit, every leadership decision, and every ministry schedule. What's the motivation behind what I do in ministry? Are we diligently prioritizing the needs of others?

LEARN to Encounter Jesus

Remember the scene from the upper room. In one of the most poignant moments before Calvary, Jesus took a basin of water and a towel and washed the disciples' feet. The Creator of the universe bowed with ultimate humility and served.

Imagine that you are in that upper room. You have been called by Jesus as one of His followers. The Savior bows before you and washes your feet. Imagine the humility on display as the One without sin stoops before you and washes dirt from your feet. Reflect on this scene. How you would feel?

Jesus, when I imagine receiving such an important gift from you, I feel...

Why did Jesus spend some of His final, precious moments washing feet? Why would Christ want to do the same for us? John 13:15 gives us the answer: "I have given you an example to follow. Do as I have done to you." Christ's agenda is clear. He gives the example and then asks us to follow it.

Spend the next few moments asking God to reveal the people who could benefit from your humble service. Picture yourself kneeling beside the Savior and humbly serving the ones He shows you.

Jesus, who needs more of my humility? Who needs more of my service? Show me the faces of the ones who need me to kneel before them and serve alongside you. Show me, Lord. I'm listening...

DILIGENCE IN PRIORITY OF MARRIAGE AND FAMILY

Marriage and family are to be a major focus for the pastor and church leader. In order to have a successful ministry, one must have a growing, vibrant relationship with one's spouse and family. No matter how popular a pastor may be with people or how effective the preaching, if he is not committed to a thriving marriage and family relationship, ministry will not endure. What is needed for a healthy, growing marriage? Scripture helps us know where to begin: "Each individual among you also is to *love his own wife* even as himself, and the wife must see to it that she *respects her husband*" (Ephesians 5:33).

We must move beyond just a rational understanding of truth to a relational expression of truth in marriage and family. Are you expressing unconditional love to your spouse? To your children? Are you giving proper respect to one another by placing your spouse and family before a ministry schedule? Gratefully, the same grace that saves our souls can also rescue our marriages and families.

➤ LOVE Others in Community

Make time to express your humility and love. Ask this question of both your spouse and your family:

I want you to sense that you are the most important people in my life. I want to know how I can improve because I love you so much. In order for you to sense my priority, what would you enjoy more of or less of from me?

✚ SHARE with Others in Community

Talk to another person about how Jesus has reset your priorities, your thought life, or your ministry mind-set. Your words might begin like these:

> *Jesus has made a difference in the priorities of my life. I now…*
> *Jesus has made some changes in how I see my role in ministry. I now…*
> *Jesus has changed the way I think about things. I used to… but now…*

11

I want to see the gospel address abortion and increase our deliberate care for children, especially through adoption and foster care. Let the well-being of children be among our highest priorities.

Jesus, reset my prayer life.

Our Savior's love is so big, sometimes it's hard to fathom the greatness of His love. Here is one aspect of Jesus' love that might have slipped your notice. Even when Christ faced impending death, He was still meeting needs. In John 13, Jesus invited the disciples into a divine relationship with Him, to "belong" to Him (v. 8). In John 14, Christ reassured His followers of His care and His provision: "No, I will not abandon you as orphans—I will come to you" (v. 18), and the Holy Spirit who "lives with you now... later will be in you" (v. 17). In the next chapter, Jesus disclosed, "You didn't choose me. I chose you" (John 15:16). And then out of His want-us-to-belong, never-ever-abandon-us heart, Jesus prayed the high priestly prayer of John 17. The Savior was about to die, and yet He was still sensitive to the vulnerable needs of His friends. What does this mean for us?

The book of James tells us plainly. Our commitment to care for those in need is a litmus test of our relationship with God. "Pure and genuine religion in the sight of God the Father means caring for orphans and widows in their distress" (James 1:27).

BECOMING HOME

From Becoming Home: Adoption, Foster Care, and Mentoring
by Jedd Medefind

More than 150 million children worldwide meet the definition of orphan, with at least one parent dead. It's a staggering figure, one that's difficult to fathom. But imagine it like this: that is enough children to fill 180 professional football stadiums. And beyond the numbers are very real situations.

There is no doubt the Bible carries a clear mandate to care for orphans. But caring for orphans is not mandate alone. It is foremost a mirror of God's heart. The prophet Hosea told Israel to say to God, "In you the fatherless find compassion" (Hosea 14:3). The Psalms express, "A father to the fatherless, a defender of widows, is God in his holy dwelling. God sets the lonely in families" (Psalm 68:5–6). But most breathtaking of all, this is not only the orphan's story. It is ours as well. For the heart of the Christian story—the gospel—is how God sought us when we were destitute and alone.

 **LEARN** to Encounter Jesus

Imagine that you are in that upper room. Jesus takes a basin of water and a towel and humbly washes your feet. He looks up at you and gently proclaims, "Remember, you're the one I love. I chose you. I couldn't bear the thought of not having a relationship with you, so I elected you as My beloved. I've seen how alone you were and how you were separated from me.

So I had to act. My death is for you—so that we can be a family—so that you belong to Me." How do you feel? Tell Him.

Jesus, when I imagine You kneeling before me and inviting me into a relationship with You, I feel...

Now do as Psalm 100:4 says: "Give thanks to Him and praise His name."

Adoption, foster care, and other ways of aiding vulnerable children represent vital engagement with a critical social justice need. But they also offer a rich theological expression of our relationship with God. Whenever and wherever we become home for the orphan, we point ultimately to an even greater reality. We are reminded that at the center of all things is the Father who pursued us at immeasurable cost to himself—who now welcomes us home as his daughters and sons.

CARING TRANSFORMS CHILDREN

Love and belonging change the trajectory of a child's life, from foster care to support of widow-and-orphan families. Despite the special challenges that can come with adoption, research consistently shows that adopted children thrive in loving homes. Even when children adopted from difficult backgrounds struggle, studies show they fare far better than orphaned peers who were never adopted.

CARING TRANSFORMS INDIVIDUALS AND FAMILIES

Children transform through adoption and foster care, but families are changed even more. As we encounter Jesus in the destitute child, Christians are pulled beyond a flaccid, self-focused religion to a costly-but-muscular faith. Coming to grasp God's heart for the fatherless begins to change us. When we hear from Scripture that God is especially tender and near to the destitute child, we start to hope that He might be willing to come near to us too. And when we see God's love for orphans reflected by His people in real, tangible ways, we begin to be able to believe it all might be true.

CARING TRANSFORMS CHURCHES

Love for orphans transforms churches as well. It helps us to see God's true character more than any sermon. Caring for orphans is an undertaking for the entire church community to engage together. Not every Christian is called to foster or adopt. But every Christian community is called to embody the pure religion that includes caring for orphans and widows in their distress. No other institution in the world is capable of embracing orphans and supporting their families like the local church. As we support each other amid the joys and struggles of loving children from difficult places, we are knit ever closer as community. Imagine the church defined by this—not primarily by what we oppose, but by a rare and profligate hospitality for children the world often discards.

Foster care, adoption, and other ways of loving orphans call the entire church community to embrace children together. It's about the family of God becoming home to those who ache for one. This can be acted out in ways large and small. Young adults can offer babysitting to give adoptive and foster parents a break. Empty nesters can run errands and help with yard care. A mechanic could teach foster youth simple car maintenance. Hairstylists might offer free haircuts every other month. Others can just invite over for a BBQ "the extra-large family" or "the family with special needs." All these acts can make a world of difference practically. They also convey something even more valuable to both parent and child: You are most welcome here.

PRAY and Experience Scripture

"We love each other because he loved us first." (1 John 4:19)

Pray now for the needs of orphaned children both near and far. Pray that Christians would rise as the answer for each child's need. With humility and attentiveness to the Lord's voice, ask God what role He may have for you in that.

Jesus, You have loved me when I was alone and destitute in my sin. I am so grateful because…

Please speak to me about the role that you might want me to have in the care for orphans. I want to love because You loved me first. Speak Lord, I am listening…

Prompt Your followers to rise up and meet the needs of children.

CARING TRANSFORMS A WATCHING WORLD

Love for orphans transforms our world, as it sees—perhaps for the first time—the gospel embodied. Another pastor, Daniel Bennett, helped his church in Illinois start a foster and adoption ministry. He saw it not only as a "justice ministry" but also as a venture of both discipleship and evangelism. Daniel describes what is happening now: "As our church grows excited about orphan ministry, I see people coming to grasp the love of God more deeply. I also see it growing our understanding of biblical love—that it involves real sacrifice; it gives like God does to those who have no way to pay you back." This countercultural hospitality for hurting children reverberates beyond the church. Daniel goes on: "People outside our church who you never would have expected are intrigued, asking questions, because they're seeing the adoptions and care for the foster kids. It really gives the church a more powerful testimony to the community."

The apologist Tertullian wrote, "It is our care for the helpless, our practice of loving kindness, that brands us in the eyes of many of our opponents."

✚ SHARE with Others in Community

Talk to a friend, family member, or ministry leader about your relationship with Jesus and how He has become a "home" for you. Tell the story of your adoption into God's family and what that's meant to you.

I am so grateful to have a relationship with Jesus. He has been my "family" even when…

➤ LOVE Others in Community

Look for a way to practically support the adoption and foster care ministry in your church/community. Plan to contribute in one or more of these ways: financial support, helping adoptive families with travel needs, assisting an adoptive family with household tasks, starting or serving an adoption support group, or becoming an adoptive or foster parent yourself!

I sense that the Lord wants me to care for orphans by…

12

I want to see more examples of righteous relationships around me. I want my relationships to be pleasing to You most of all!

Jesus, reset my prayer life.

Our righteousness and holiness are of paramount importance to Jesus. His final prayer with the disciples emphasized this truth. Jesus asked the Father, "Make them holy by your truth... And I give myself as a holy sacrifice for them so they can be made holy by your truth" (John 17:17–19). Christ chose to pray for our holiness in the final hours of His life, therefore it must be important! Christ's prayer not only reveals the priority of our Savior; it gives us the key to righteousness in our own relationships. Sacrifice.

WHAT'S LOVE GOT TO DO WITH IT?

From 10 *Ways to Say* "I *Love You*"
by Josh McDowell

In 1984, musical artist Tina Turner released the hit song, "What's Love Got to Do with It?" It portrayed two people trying to have a relationship based on the physical. That relationship priority simply doesn't work for the long haul. But when you truly understand what love is and pursue a true love for a person, not just a body, it can be the most rewarding experience in life for a lifetime.

A lot of people can tell you what love *does* and how it behaves, but they can't tell you *what it is*. For example, people know the Bible says that love acts patiently and is kind. It says love isn't "jealous or boastful or proud or rude. It does not demand its own way" (1 Corinthians 13:4–5). That's the way love operates, but what is love exactly? What is the motivating factor of love?

Jesus identified the motivating factor when he said, "Do to others whatever you would like them to do to you" (Matthew 7:12). The apostle Paul described love this way: "In humility, value others above yourselves, not looking to your own interest but each of you to the interests of others" (Philippians 2:4 NIV). In other words, real love is other-focused.

With these and other verses, we can define what real love is. *Real love*, a love that is other-focused, *makes the security, happiness, and welfare of another person as important as your own.*

💬 PRAY and Experience Scripture

Quietly ask the Lord to remind and encourage you in the ways you have demonstrated real love to those around you.

Lord, remind me of some of the ways I have loved my spouse/family/friends in ways that look like Your real love. When have they been able to see that I am trying to serve You? When would they have noticed that I have treated them like You would want to be treated?

Celebrate these remembrances with gratitude toward the Lord. Tell Jesus about your gladness. Then ask His Spirit to show you how you can serve Jesus by demonstrating even more love to your spouse/family/loved ones and other Jesus followers.

Lord, show me new ways to love the special people in my life. Show me areas where I can take even more initiative to serve my spouse/family/loved ones. Show me how You might even want me to sacrifice for them.

Listen quietly and yield to whatever Jesus has to say.

In order to love your spouse or that special person in your life, you need to know and accept why God loves and accepts you.

As a being created by God, you are worthy of love for at least three reasons:

1. *God created you lovable.* If you grew up feeling ignored, unwanted, or even despised, the people who conveyed that self-image to you were dead wrong. God makes no mistakes. You are lovable because He created you in His image—a lovable, relational image. Your lovability has been placed in your relational DNA by God Himself.

2. *God created you valuable.* Anyone who says to you that you are not worth much or are unimportant is deluded. Remember, you are valuable because you were created by God in His very image. He is eternally valuable, and He has made you valuable too.

    You see, the value of an item is determined by what someone is willing to sacrifice or exchange for it. What was your worth to God? It was the sacrificial death of His only Son. He sent His Son in the form of a human to purchase you back. He considers you worth dying for so He can have a relationship with you.

3. *God created you competent.* Perhaps you were always the last person to complete an important task or to be chosen for a team sport. As a result, you may view yourself as incompetent or lacking great potential. But God doesn't see you that way. If you are His child, He has given you special talents and gifts. He has placed His Holy Spirit within you to empower you for service. You are far from incompetent or lacking giftedness. Since God has entrusted you with special gifts and empowered you with His Spirit, you can count on it: you are competent.

The more clearly you see yourself as lovable, valuable, and competent, the better equipped you are to unselfishly love. Our vision of ourselves even gets clearer when we embrace the truth of how God sees us. Let's experience how He sees us.

LEARN to Encounter Jesus

"But God demonstrates his own love for us in this: While we were still sinners, Christ died for us." (Romans 5:8 NIV)

God declared our infinite, unconditional worth at Calvary. Pause to allow His Spirit to overwhelm you with the wonder of His love—unmerited, unstoppable, unlimited grace. Imagine that Jesus is sitting beside you. Listen to the words that are just for You.

Precious child of mine, I have great news: My love has no conditions or limits. There's nothing you can do to earn my love. There's nothing you can do to lose my love. There's no expiration date, no hoops to jump through or requirements to fulfill. I love you. Period. The good news is that this love is my gift—all you have to do is accept it.

Finish this moment of prayer by voicing your thankfulness to the Savior.

Jesus, when I read about Your love, my heart feels so grateful because…

Let's be clear. If we're praying for righteousness, we certainly need righteousness in our romantic relationships. Therefore, we need to talk about sex. How does it fit in?

God's "other-focused" formula still applies. Here's how: when your spouse truly makes your security, happiness, and welfare as important as his own, it touches you deeply and revs your engine sexually. The mark of a fantastic lover is the underlying motivation—to give to you, to please you, and to satisfy your every need because you are you. Your lover's fascination with the inner you provides substance and depth to any sexual response. When other-focused love sees sex as an expression of providing and protecting love, a fantastic lover is born.

Remember, your pursuit of intimacy goes both ways. You'll have to choose to know the person you love—really know him or her. Discover the dreams, hopes, fears, and joys of his or her life. Understand his or her relational needs and move in to meet those needs. You will also have to choose to allow your lover to know you. Open up, be vulnerable, and share who you are—your hopes, dreams, joys, and fears. Be transparent about your relational needs and allow your lover to move into your life and meet those needs. And finally, choose to enter the world of your lover and be caringly involved in his or her interests. Make those interests your own and journey through life together. This is the proven way to relational intimacy. This is truly the secret to loving.

✛ SHARE with Others in Community

Make plans to share your own story of sacrifice, others-focused love, and righteousness in relationships. Think about how Jesus has reset your relationships—how His sacrifice has produced a measure of righteousness in you. Then similarly, tell how your sacrifice (and less focus on yourself) has produced positive things in your relationships. Your story might begin with these words:

I used to think only about myself and my needs in relationships. Jesus changed a lot of that. Because of His sacrifice, I've learned that My relationships are now different because…

LOVE Others in Community

"Freely you have received; freely give." (Matthew 10:8 NIV)

Righteous relationships begin when we stop focusing on, "What am I getting out of this relationship?" and rather focus on, "How am I giving?" Loving others with sacrifice and initiative is a critical part of righteous relationships.

Follow Jesus' example: Pray and live out this request:

Heavenly Father, I want to be a better "giver" to my spouse/family/ loved one. Help me lift my focus beyond myself to notice the needs of others. Prompt my mind and empower my initiative to meet these needs. Empower my sacrifice, just like You have sacrificed for me.

SECTION 4

MY SPIRIT-EMPOWERED FAITH

will mean that I love His mission through expressing and extending the kingdom of God as compassion, justice, love, and forgiveness are shared.

As I practice this outcome, I will become a champion of Jesus in my community and culture.

Listen as Jesus prays for you to be engaged in the world as His ambassador, confident of His protection from evil.

> **Jesus looked up to heaven and said,**
> **"Father, I'm not asking you to take them out of the**
> **world, but to keep them safe from the evil one.**
> **Just as you sent me into the world, I am sending**
> **them into the world."** John 17:15, 18

Now pray *with* Jesus. Join the prayer meeting that He is already leading on your behalf. *Jesus, please reset my prayer life.*

- I want to see my community and our nation's leaders look to the church for the answer to society's problems.

- I want to see Your influence restored to the arts, media, and communication in our communities.

- I want to see my neighborhood transformed. Let there be more expressions of love, more serving of one another, more demonstrations of compassion, and more evidence of unity.

- I pray for an increase in care for the homeless and the hungry in our communities. Jesus, let my vertical faith in You meet the horizontal needs of the most vulnerable people around me.

13

I want to see my community and our nation's leaders look to the church for the answer to society's problems.

Jesus, reset my prayer life.

The political and societal landscape of our communities can often look hopeless. It's not hard to find fault with many of our leaders. How should we respond? How can we position ourselves as intercessors for the leaders we may never meet? The story of Daniel provides a perfect example. Daniel served his country valiantly. Even his enemies determined that Daniel was completely trustworthy. Consequently, the only grounds of accusation they could find related to Daniel's religion. His enemies executed a wicked scheme, and Daniel found himself in a den of lions because of his faithfulness to the living God. Daniel's life angered most of the political leaders, but the king's response tells us that Daniel's integrity did not go unnoticed. Having observed Daniel's life of integrity and commitment to His God, the king actually hoped that Daniel's life was saved. One man's example of living faith turned the heart of a king.

Thousands of years ago, Jesus confirmed the truth of our day: "The world's sin is that it refuses to believe in me" (John 16:9). Many of our leaders refuse to believe in Jesus. So how do we now pray? First, we too must live a life of integrity and commitment to our God. And then we pray Christ's prayer in John 16. We rest assured that "when He comes, He will convict the world of its sin, and of God's righteousness…" (John 16:8). We pray that the Holy Spirit would convict hearts and point our leaders to the one true God as we live as modern-day "Daniels," living so that our faith will turn the hearts of kings.

EXTEND THE KINGDOM

From *The Circle Maker*

by Mark Batterson

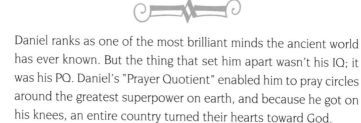

Daniel ranks as one of the most brilliant minds the ancient world has ever known. But the thing that set him apart wasn't his IQ; it was his PQ. Daniel's "Prayer Quotient" enabled him to pray circles around the greatest superpower on earth, and because he got on his knees, an entire country turned their hearts toward God.

Daniel didn't just pray when he had a bad day; he prayed every day. He didn't just dial up 911 prayers when he was in a lions' den; prayer was part of the rhythm and routine of his life. Prayer was his life, and his life was a prayer. I'm sure Daniel prayed with a greater degree of intensity right before he was thrown into the lions' den, but that intensity was the by-product of consistency. And it was **this consistent prayer** that **led to one of the most unlikely rises to power in political history. How does a prisoner of war become prime minister of the country that took him captive in the first place?**

Only God. The ascendance of Daniel defies political science, but it defines the power of prayer circles. Prayer invites God into the equation, and when that happens, all bets are off. It doesn't matter whether it's the locker room, the boardroom, or the classroom. If you *stop, drop, and pray*, then you never know where you'll go, what you'll do, or who you'll meet.

Prayer puts us in a spiritual frame of mind. Prayer helps us see and seize the God-ordained opportunities that are all around us all the time. Daniel was so primed with prayer that it didn't just sanctify his subconscious; it gave him supernatural discernment with King Nebuchadnezzar. Daniel discerned the king's dream because he could read his mind. *It's almost as though prayer gives us a sixth sense!*

Somewhere near the intersection of science and spirituality is a paradigm-shifting principle best seen in the exercise practiced by King David: "In the morning, LORD, you hear my voice; in the morning I lay my requests before you and wait expectantly" (Psalm 5:3).

LEARN to Encounter Jesus

We know that Christ is available to talk with us in prayer— yet our homes, workplaces, and communities sometimes show little evidence of His presence.

Consider your own life: In what areas do you need to experience more of His presence through prayer? Be still before the Lord, inviting Him to speak to you. After you've heard from Him, complete the following sentence:

Lord Jesus, I sense that I need to pray to You more often about:

- my relationships with family members and friends.
- my workplace or community.
- my thoughts and attitudes.
- my words.
- my emotions.
- my choices.

- prayer, solitude, and meditation.
- worship and Bible study.
- my witness and lifestyle.
- Other: _____.

Share your responses with the Lord.

Lord Jesus, I sense that I need to pray to You more often in my…

For example: *Lord Jesus, I sense that I need to depend on You more in my financial choices. I tend to make decisions without really praying for Your guidance.*

Here's the good news: "If we ask anything according to his will, he hears us. And if we know that he hears us—whatever we ask—we know that we have what we asked of him" (1 John 5:14–15 NIV).

EVERY MIRACLE HAS A GENESIS MOMENT.

In the first century BC, it was a circle in the sand drawn by a sage named Honi. For Moses, it was declaring that God would provide meat to eat in the middle of nowhere, even though he had no idea how. For Elijah, it was getting on his knees seven times and praying for rain. For Daniel, I think it traces back to one resolution.

Along with daily decisions, there are defining decisions. We only make a few defining decisions in life, and then we spend the rest of our lives managing them. Maybe you've made some bad decisions that have gotten you to where you don't want to be. The good news is that you're only one defining decision away from a totally different life. Let's reset your destiny. You could be the answer to specific needs in the culture, just like Daniel. Let this exercise help reset some of your defining decisions.

PRAY and Experience Scripture

"Each of you should use whatever gift you have received to serve others, as faithful stewards of God's grace in its various forms." (1 Peter 4:10 NIV)

This passage in 1 Peter reminds us that the various dimensions or forms of God's grace can be "administered," or served, to others. Some of the dimensions of God's grace include His encouragement, His comfort, His support, His kindness, His honor/approval, His attentiveness, and many others. Consider your life and the gifts you have generously received from God. Have you received a large dose of His kindness, encouragement, comfort, attentiveness, or approval?

- Ask the Lord to remind you of a specific aspect of grace that has been showered upon you.

  God, as I reflect on all the aspects of your grace, I know that You have given me an especially large "dose" of Your... I'm grateful to have received Your grace because of my...

  For example: God, I know that You have given me an especially large dose of Your attentiveness. You've reassured me that the smallest details of my life are noticed by You. There have been so many times that You've confirmed Your care.

- Next, reflect on some of the ways in which you (and possibly other members of your church) can give this aspect of grace to others. Pause to listen to the Lord.

> • Now make a decision—a decision that could define your destiny and the destiny of your church. Name the specific aspect of grace that could be shared with others.
>
> *I want to share more of Jesus with my community and show them that Jesus is the answer to our community's problems. Therefore, I resolve to give…*

Daniel makes one of these defining decisions as a teenager. It doesn't seem like a big deal, but it changes the course of his story and history. Daniel's ascent to power traces all the way back to one resolution. Daniel *resolved not to defile himself with the royal food and wine.*

Daniel risked his reputation by refusing the royal food. It was an insult to the king, but Daniel was more concerned about insulting God. Daniel knew it would violate Jewish dietary laws, and while that may not seem like a big deal, if you obey God in the little things, then God knows He can use you to do big things! It was Daniel's unwillingness to compromise his convictions in the little things that led to his big break. Daniel did a ten-day fast that won him favor with the king's chief official, and that favor translated into his first job with the administration. Then "the favor of him who dwelt in the burning bush" kept opening doors via a series of promotions until Daniel was second-in-command to the king.

I wonder if Daniel ever had one of those out-of-the-spirit moments when he looked in the mirror and asked himself, "How did I get here?" The answer: *daily decisions and defining decisions.* Never underestimate the potential of one resolution to change your life. It can be a genesis moment. Daniel's destiny traces all the way back to one resolution not to defile himself, but making the resolution was easier than keeping it. That is where prayer, coupled with fasting, comes into play.

→ **LOVE Others in Community**

"Give as freely as you have received." (Matthew 10:8)

Continue your resolution by defining *how* and to *whom* you will give. In what ways have you freely received from God, and now how does He want you to freely give to others? Could there be someone in your life or in your community who could benefit from your good stewardship of God's riches? Ask the Lord to speak to you about a specific person or group of people:

Jesus, show me how to share more of what You have freely given to me. Show me the person or group of people with whom you want me to share…

Then complete the following sentences:

Jesus, I sense that you want me to share some of your _____ (kindness, encouragement, comfort, support, attentiveness, approval)

with _____ (name a specific person or group of people)

by _____ (name the specific way you will share this aspect of God's grace).

✚ SHARE with Others in Community

Make plans to tell your story of grace to others. Also make plans to share your resolution. Your words might begin like these:

Your story of grace:

I *have received the most amazing gift from Jesus. He has given me a huge dose of His…*
And *this has made a difference in my life because…*

Your resolution:

I *am so grateful for the grace that Jesus has given to me that I want to share it with others. I've decided to make a difference in our community by…*

14

I *want to see* Your *influence restored to the arts, media, and communication in our communities.*

Jesus, reset my prayer life.

There's some good news and some bad news about our time here on earth. In Christ's final prayer in the upper room, He reminds us of the bad news: We're in a world that's less than perfect. We're here with the evil one, in a place where others hate us. Read the Savior's prayer: "I have given them your word. And the world hates them because they do not belong to the world, just as I do not belong to the world. I'm not asking you to take them out of the world, but to keep them safe from the evil one" (John 17:14–15). The good news came a chapter earlier when Jesus reminded all of us, "But take heart, because I have overcome the world" (John 16:33). We're often painfully aware of the world that's less than perfect, but since Christ has overcome, how do we thrive while we're here? Perhaps, if we let Jesus impact our choices in this world, we'll see more of His protection and provision.

A CURIOUS CORRELATION

From *The Politically Incorrect Jesus*
by Joe Battaglia

There's a fascinating correlation between how we nourish and satisfy the part of us that appreciates and even requires a creative interaction with our environments, such as our entertainment choices, and our own personal growth as individuals. **How we ultimately treat each other is an outward expression of how we inwardly feel about ourselves.** And how we feel about ourselves and how we understand our world is often a function of what we "ingest" in our entertainment choices and the news we consume.

The kind of programming we ingest into our minds will often dictate what we eliminate from our mouths. A diet of information that denigrates rather than elevates the human spirit will find its way out in what we say and do.

And when that happens, we see that acted out in our culture. There is more fear. More insecurity. More lack of civility.

 **LEARN** to Encounter Jesus

Take the next few moments to pause for prayer. Listen to the Holy Spirit's voice as He speaks to you about your own choices of entertainment and how these choices might give rise to:

- Increased fears—what fears, anxieties, or uncertainties are often prompted in you?
- Unhealthy relationships—what relationships might hinder your full expression of Jesus' love?
- Unhealthy emotions/patterns—what patterns of anger, selfishness, busyness, or pride might be impacting how you treat other people?

Meditate quietly on Calvary and the choice of Jesus. Jesus chose love because of how He feels about you!

Now consider praying a prayer of humility: *Lord Jesus, free me from anything that distracts me from You. Liberate me from fears or even relationships that hinder me from expressing Your love. Free me from all these things so that I can better express your love to people around me.*

Galatians 5:13 reminds us, "For you have been called to live in freedom, my brothers and sisters. But don't use your freedom to satisfy your sinful nature. Instead, use your freedom to serve one another in love." Pray this Scripture with Jesus.

Jesus, you have called me into a relationship with You. That relationship is marked by freedom. But I also know that You don't want me to use this freedom for things that aren't honoring to You. So help me make entertainment choices that are both honoring to You and that encourage me to serve others in love.

WHY HAS THIS HAPPENED?

I believe the politically correct notion of eliminating the idea of absolutes has contributed to this downfall. If there is no right and wrong, everyone's opinions and ideas are as true and valuable to society as everyone else's. Once we eliminate the notion of what's good or bad, the slippery slope of what people will do and tolerate becomes more acceptable.

As a trained journalist, I always understood my job to observe and interpret the news. Unfortunately, that's all changed, it seems. We've exchanged information and observation for titillation. We've become a nation of voyeurs, people who are content to sit and gawk at others' lives. We no longer have any sense of shame, because we're told there's nothing to be ashamed of anymore.

So we are content to live vicariously through others, regardless of how insipid, mean, banal, or fruitless the participants are or what they do. Fame is to be celebrated above all else. We can watch others cheat on their spouses, have children out of wedlock, have meltdowns in their homes, and denigrate others openly and joyously. Then awards are handed out to the people and shows that celebrate all these things.

This is the new entertainment. It appeals to the lowest common denominator or prurient interest in man rather than aspiring to explore our higher, more noble essence with content that reaches for the stars. Now we glorify the villains and vilify the glorious. We create celebrities of those who have no gift, no talent, no redeeming elements to their lives other than to belittle others and themselves in the process.

A constant diet of the type of entertainment we consume kicks in the desire to be like those we watch. If we feed on programs that belittle or breed insecurity, we can embrace those attributes, becoming insecure and belittling ourselves. As we unknowingly internalize the character qualities uplifted, they ultimately come out in our behavior.

We've gorged ourselves on what is destructive and violent and have created a culture of violence. Because we've laughed at the shows that belittle and denigrate, there are more incidents of acting out scenarios of bullying and meanness in the public square than ever before.

We've decided it's okay to put on pedestals those who cheat, connive to get ahead, or lie to their spouses and friends. But we watch and wonder why our families are disintegrating, leaving behind the carnage of broken children. Then we ponder anew when those broken children grow up and decide to act out their fear and insecurity with violence—sometimes with their fists, but all too often with a handy weapon of choice. The tragic results of what our culture has produced are littered around us.

Though we have aimed for the lowest common denominator of entertainment, we moan when we find that played out in how people actually treat each other and how our businesses treat their customers.

PRAY and Experience Scripture

"The gates of [hell] shall not prevail…" (Matthew 16:18 NKJV)

Take a moment to brainstorm a list of ten to fifteen "enemies" that seem to be attacking our homes and relationships today (i.e. divorce, addictions, debt, healthcare, etc.).

Now, remember a time when you intentionally increased the amount of relational support and connectedness in your home, in your friendships, or in your small group. Reflect on this correlation: How did this increase in support help you become more successful in facing and overcoming these enemy attacks?

> I *remember when my home/friends faced* _____
> *and we* _____ *when the attacks came. We were*
> *able to get through this struggle because we supported each other well.*
>
> Now pause to pray—believing God for His prevailing
> power and claiming the promise that His people will overcome.

WHAT GOES IN...?

The apostle Paul knew all too well the indigestion of entertainment when he told us: "Whatever is true, whatever is noble,
whatever is right, whatever is pure, whatever is lovely, whatever is
admirable—if anything is excellent or praiseworthy—think about
such things" (Philippians 4:8). He understood this universal truth:
what goes in will ultimately come out.

I learned long ago that my mind doesn't have to be a repos-
itory for someone else's garbage. Nor should yours be. We reap
what we sow.

So watch out what entertains you. The drama you vicariously
see and enjoy on the screen may one day be yours experientially
to share in.

✚ SHARE with Others in Community

Reflect on your own experiences. How have you noticed
a correlation between what goes into your mind and what
comes out? Now reflect on the difference that Jesus makes in
your choices. Plan to share your story with another person.
Your conversation might begin with these words:

> *I know that my choices about entertainment affect me because…*
> *But Jesus has reset my choices. I now…*

→ LOVE Others in Community

"A new commandment I give to you, that you love one another; as I have loved you…" (John 13:34 NKJV)

Think about your extended family, coworkers, neighbors, and friends.

- Who is facing attacks from the enemy and could benefit from your support?
- Who is facing a series of difficult circumstances in life and could benefit from your encouragement and comfort?
- Who has specific financial or tangible needs and could benefit from your giving?

Pray and ask God to bring specific people to your mind as you consider each question above. Talk with your spouse, family member, or close friend about how you plan to follow through on helping to remove the aloneness of others.

15

I want to see my neighborhood transformed.
Let there be more expressions of love, more
serving of one another, more demonstrations
of compassion, and more evidence of unity.

Jesus, reset my prayer life.

Christ's reputation as a healer and teacher spread across the country. So as He rode a small donkey down the winding trails, people began to recognize Him. A crowd gathered and joyfully began to praise God. For the first time in ministry, Jesus was publicly praised. Then something odd occurred. He reached a certain point on the path to Jerusalem and began to cry. Cry? On a festive occasion such as this, what would prompt the Savior to cry? (See Luke 19:41–44.)

TOWARD NEIGHBORHOOD TRANSFORMATION: HOW TO LIVE IN A PRAYED-FOR NEIGHBORHOOD

From *Toward Neighborhood Transformation*
by Steve Hawthorne

Jesus *looked upon* Jerusalem—past her regal palace, past her standing as a strong military force and hub of commerce. Jesus looked past all that and saw the people. He came upon the city, saw the people's hurt, and His heart's response was to cry. How do our hearts respond when we look upon our neighborhood? What might happen in our city if we allowed our hearts to be moved with the same compassion?

NEIGHBORHOOD TRANSFORMATION

I love knowing that God is already at work in my neighborhood. God has been doing good things constantly, every passing day, in the life of every breathing person. Of course, most of what God does for people goes unnoticed. He is not recognized for most of the kindness and life that He bestows. But that's not the way God wants it. And that's not how it will be. The Bible resounds with promise that ultimately, the risen Lord will be known, loved, and followed by some in every people. When God-lovers become neighbor-lovers, the community changes in tangible ways. It's what some people have called transformation.

GOD'S GLORY IN A PRAYED-FOR NEIGHBORHOOD

Can you imagine living in a prayed-for city? It would be a community in which every person is being prayed for in Jesus' name by caring Christian neighbors. How much room would God have to work when people come to know that they are being prayed for? If anything good happens, people would likely give God at least partial credit. If anything drastic or difficult happened, I think people would look in God's direction for help.

Can you imagine yourself living in a prayed-for neighborhood? Why not envision every person in your neighborhood being prayed for? You can aim to fill your neighborhood, campus, or workplace with prayer. Anyone can do it. Here's how:

PRAYER WALKING: GET CLOSER TO PRAY CLEARER

Prayer walking is praying near the people you are praying for, in the places where they live or work. Prayer walking isn't really about walking around. *It's praying with your eyes and heart wide open* so you can take notice of what God may want to do in their lives. You can pray quietly with your eyes open without people necessarily knowing that you are praying for them. Be on the scene without making one.

LEARN to Encounter Jesus

Just like in Jerusalem (in Luke 19), what if Jesus was to "look upon" your home? What would He feel when He saw the struggles of your family? Because Jesus is the same yesterday, today, and forever, we can be confident that just as He felt compassion for Jerusalem, He feels compassion for you! The writer of Hebrews reminds us that Jesus not only feels compassion for our needs, but He is in heaven, constantly interceding for us (Hebrews 7:25). Picture this moment: Christ is praying for your marriage, your family, and your friends out of a compassionate, tender heart. Picture the image of Jesus leaning over and whispering a prayer to the Father. You hear Him praying for the needs of your life from a heart of kindness and care.

What does it do to your heart to know that Jesus loves you so much that the needs of your life move Him with compassion? Then out of compassion, He intercedes for you?

Jesus, when I consider that You are praying for me—because you feel compassion and care for me—it brings _____ to my heart.

(For example: *joy, peace, gladness, thanks, excitement, awe,* or *wonder*)

Tell Jesus about your thanksgiving and praise.

PRAY GOD'S PURPOSE: PRAY SCRIPTURE

If you learn how to pray Scripture, you don't really need to know what your neighbors' specific needs or requests might be. Begin by thanking God for the good things that He has already done. We are urged to offer "thanksgiving on behalf of all people" (1 Timothy 2:1). You can be sure of this: God has been "under-thanked" in your community. As you read the stories, songs, and promises of Scripture, try to give God honor for doing some things in the lives of people near you.

Use those same bits of Scripture as the substance of what you pray. Learn the art of paraphrasing (or prayer-a-phrasing) promises or stories of the Bible into prayers that use your own words. Make it your focus to pray toward what God desires to bring about in their lives. Pray for His intended destiny for the community. Essentially, if you pray in hope, you will find yourself praying with love. Take a few moments to pray right now.

PRAY and Experience Scripture

"So will My word be which goes forth from My mouth; it will not return to Me empty, without accomplishing what I desire…" (Isaiah 55:11 NASB).

Prayerfully reflect on the verses below as part of God's hope for your community. Pray for your neighborhood that God's Word will not return empty.

- "What does the Lord require of you but to do justice, to love kindness, and to walk humbly with your God?" (Micah 6:8 NASB)
- "'To the extent that you did it to one of these brothers of Mine, even the least of them, you did it to Me.'" (Matthew 25:40 NASB)
- "He will restore the hearts of the fathers to their children and the hearts of the children to their fathers…" (Malachi 4:6 NASB)
- "For this is the will of God, your sanctification; that is, that you abstain from sexual immorality…" (1 Thessalonians 4:3–5 NASB)
- "And He said to him, "'You shall love the Lord your God with all your heart, and with all your soul, and with all your mind.' This is the great and foremost commandment. The second is like it, 'You shall love your neighbor as yourself.'" (Matthew 22:37–40 NASB)
- "Go therefore and make disciples of all the nations … teaching them to observe all that I commanded you…" (Matthew 28:19–20 NASB)

PRAY YOUR WAY INTO THEIR STORY:
FROM PRAYER TO CARE TO SHARE

People who persistently pray with thanks and in biblical hope often find that God inspires them with creative ways to express simple kindness to their neighbors. Small gestures of kindness are themselves the very blessing that God promised would flow from Abraham's family (Genesis 12:2–3, 22:18). These kinds of simple acts are the substance of the neighbor love that God commands (Mark 12:29–31). But there's more. Such tangible kindness often throws open ways to communicate the gospel in sensitive, relevant clarity. Persistent, life-giving prayer for others leads to opportunities to care, displaying God's love, which opens the way to share the gospel, declaring God's love.

Coming soon: Some of the best things that God will ever do in history.

I think it's highly likely that many of us will soon be living in prayed-for cities. I'm stretching my heart to believe that we will someday be living in a prayed-for world. That's going to be a world in which God gets tremendous glory.

✚ SHARE with Others in Community

Plan now to share your story of how Jesus has made a difference in your life. Talk to a neighbor, friend, or colleague about what Jesus has done and the hope that He offers.

First, reflect on the lives of your friends and neighbors. What do you see when you "look upon" their lives?

Do they need acceptance, compassion, peace, confidence, discernment, forgiveness, restoration, or provision? Now, reflect on all the ways that Jesus has given these same things to you. Out of gratitude for what Jesus has done for you, ask Him to give you an opportunity to share your story:

> I feel a lot of compassion for you and care about what you're going through. Especially how...
>
> It seems like you might need some _____ (acceptance, compassion, peace, etc.) right now.
>
> I've needed _____ in my life too. The person who's given me _____ is Jesus. Here's what He did...

LOVE Others in Community

Now reflect on your gratitude again and ask the Lord to empower you to show love to this same friend, family member, or neighbor in a specific, relevant way.

> God, show me how to express love to _____ (name a specific person) in a way that meets this same need for _____ (acceptance, compassion, peace, etc.)

16

I pray for an increase in care for the homeless and the hungry in our communities. Jesus, let my vertical faith in You meet the horizontal needs of the most vulnerable people around me.

Jesus, reset my prayer life.

We must stand committed to a radical gospel message that marries sanctification with service. We can be certain that this is Christ's agenda since needs of people are His top priority. Listen to the Savior's very first declaration of His calling: "The Spirit of the Lord is upon me, for he has anointed me to bring Good News to the poor. He has sent me to proclaim that captives will be released, that the blind will see, that the oppressed will be set free" (Luke 4:18). When we increase care for the homeless and hungry, we reset our priorities in line with Jesus. When we help the poor and oppressed, God blesses us and those we help.

THE LAMB'S AGENDA

From *The Lamb's Agenda*
by Samuel Rodriguez

"Who do they say I am? Who do you think I am?" (Matthew 16:13–19).

This biblical passage captures one of the most transformative moments in human history. Peter revealed Jesus. Jesus revealed the church, activated the purpose, and emancipated the kingdom. Revelation always leads to activation, and activation always leads to emancipation. We need a revelation of Jesus to activate the church's purpose, as we lead a movement of righteousness and justice. We need a movement of the Lamb's agenda . . . and the Lamb's agenda is nothing other than the agenda of Christ.

The agenda of Christ is drawn from the cross of Christ. And the cross of Christ is both vertical and horizontal. Vertically, we stand connected to God, his kingdom, eternal life, divine principles, and glory. Horizontally, to our left and to our right, we exist surrounded by and revealed through relationships, family, and community. Jesus' model of ministry was revolutionary. He embraced the banished, forgave those tormented by guilt, liberated those oppressed by evil spirits, and fed the hungry. His life was the cross in action, both planes of it, vertical and horizontal.

In the same way, our vertical salvation must lead to horizontal transformation. The good news must not only be preached, it must also be lived out. So how do we live out the Lamb's agenda? We read Matthew 25 and we heed it. We read John 3:16 and acknowledge it. We cannot easily justify a Christian ministry that convenes on Sunday morning and ignores its community from Monday through Saturday. Nor can we easily justify a ministry that treats Sunday like just another day to "do good" in the community. We derive our influence in that community not from our ability to plan events and schedule speakers, not from our eagerness to distribute food and fix houses. We derive our influence from our source of enlightenment and our willingness to share that light with those around us. The good we do in the community must flow from a power beyond us. Governments can give out more food than we can and celebrities can draw more people, but only we can share the light of God in every good deed we do.

 ## LEARN to Encounter Jesus

"For he satisfies the thirsty and fills the hungry with good things." (Psalm 107:9)

For the next few moments, remember the scene from Calvary. Remember the blood that was shed and the pain that was endured for you. Remember what Jesus did ... and how He did it for you. He took your punishment; He gave His life to save yours. Tell Jesus about your gratitude for the cross.

Jesus, I don't want to ever "get over" the miracle of the cross. So thank You for...

Next, allow your heart to ask this question: *What if I could give back to Jesus? He did so much for me—what if there was some way that I could show Him a portion of my gratitude?*

Miraculously, you can! Imagine the scene from the poorest parts of your city. Imagine the people who line the streets asking for food or money, the torn clothes and the unkempt hair. Reflect on the often-invisible faces that are worn from exposure to the elements. And now imagine that Jesus stands on those same street corners and He makes this declaration:

"When you give to the least of these, you are giving to Me!" (Matthew 25:40)

Ask the Holy Spirit to speak to you about any ways you could more effectively give to the least of these—and all the while give to Him.

Jesus, am I doing all that You desire when I see the homeless in my community? I want to see Your face on those street corners. Help me give to the least of these, just as if I am giving to You!

A MATTHEW 25 MOVEMENT

There's work to be done when thirty million people live in poverty. So where do we turn for answers? We turn to the Lamb and His agenda. You see the Lamb's agenda reconciles the sanctification and covenant of John 3:16 with the service and community of Matthew 25. There is a necessary link between compassion and evangelism. Each loses value without the other. Therefore, any church or Christian ignoring the plight of their neighbors lives an incomplete gospel.

Are we anointed to build great cathedrals or multimillion-dollar ministry platforms? Are we anointed to gather thousands around us to make them feel good about themselves and give them some place to go on Sunday mornings before brunch? I don't think so. We are anointed to bring good news to the poor, freedom to the captive, and healing to the brokenhearted. In Matthew 25, Christ admonishes us to feed the hungry and clothe the needy. Yet today, unfortunately, American Christendom too often measures success by the metrics of rows filled, books sold, and dollars collected rather than by the number of souls transformed. To recalculate our metrics, we need to ask ourselves, how does God measure success? The answer is simple and can be found in Matthew 25:34–36. "'Come, you who are blessed by my Father, inherit the Kingdom prepared for you from the creation of the world. I was hungry, and you fed me. I was thirsty, and you gave me a drink. I was a stranger, and you invited me into your home...'"

PRAY and Experience Scripture

"Don't put your confidence in powerful people; there is no help for you there. But joyful are those who have the God of Israel as their helper, whose hope is in the Lord their God. He gives justice to the oppressed and food to the hungry." (Psalm 146:3, 5, 7)

Pray for Jesus to reset your agenda and the agenda of your church. Declare your confidence in God as your helper and make yourself available to help the oppressed and hungry.

Jesus, I declare that we need Your help as we address the needs of the homeless in our community. I know Your heart is to bring justice to the oppressed, so I am available to be a conduit of Your care. Show me how I can do that...

The good news is that God is pouring out a fresh anointing upon a generation. God is anointing a generation that will deliver our brothers and sisters from malnourishment and hunger, as well as from physical and spiritual poverty. He is anointing a generation to knock down the walls of racial and economic injustice. With this agenda—the Lamb's agenda—the church *can* address the social, spiritual, physical, intellectual, and communal needs of all its constituents. To do so, it must reconcile the vertical with horizontal planes of the cross. It must be committed to the nexus of the cross. The nexus of the cross is where conviction marries compassion, where the fish intersects with the bread, where truth joins hands with mercy, where we reconcile the optics of redemption with the metrics of reconciliation. The nexus is the place where a balanced soul finds its home, where faith meets action, conviction greets compassion, and the prophetic intersects with the practical. The nexus is the strongest part of the cross, the intersection of righteousness and justice, the platform where heaven touches earth, and the womb from which the Lamb's agenda flows.

✚ SHARE with Others in Community

Talk to a friend, family member, or ministry colleague about how Jesus has (or how He wants to) reset your ministry to the homeless. Talk about what it means to minister *to* Jesus as you minister to others. Your words might begin with these:

Jesus has reset my perspective about ministry to the homeless. I've come to see that…

➡ LOVE Others in Community

"In the same way, let your good deeds shine out for all to see, so that everyone will praise your heavenly Father." (Matthew 5:16)

Make plans to get involved in serving the homeless and hungry in your community.

I plan to get involved in serving the homeless and hungry in my community by…

SECTION 5

MY SPIRIT-EMPOWERED FAITH

will mean that I love His mission through pouring life into others and making disciples who, in turn, make disciples of others.

As I practice this outcome, I will join in the eternal plan of Jesus so that others will come to know Him.

Listen as Jesus prays for your continued closeness with Him and then together you are able to express His love and hope to the world around you.

> **Jesus looked up to heaven and said,**
> *"Father, I pray that they will all be one, just as you and I are one—as you are in me, Father, and I am in you. And may they be in us so that the world will believe you sent me."* John 17:21

Now pray *with* Jesus. Join the prayer meeting that He is already leading on your behalf. *Jesus, please reset my prayer life.*

- Jesus, I want to see an increase in the number of people who choose a relationship with You and are baptized as Your followers. Change my heart so I can be an active part of this vision.

- Lord, equip me as I impart faith to the children who are in my care. I stand ready to fulfill my calling as a disciple-maker in their lives.

- Jesus, we want to see more Spirit-empowered churches where there is a focus on evangelism, practical service to those in need, more evident giving among believers, and well-being among church members is evident to everyone.

- Holy Spirit, we want to see young adults, students, and children embracing the claims of Christ. Please do Your miraculous work so that more young people live and love like Jesus.

17

I want to see an increase in the number of people who choose a relationship with You and are baptized as Your followers. Change me and my heart so I can be an active part of this vision.

Jesus, reset my prayer life.

Remember back to the time when you first became a follower of Jesus. Can you remember the wonder of becoming His new creation, the joy of a newly formed relationship with the Creator? Jesus remembers that day. He remembers it because He couldn't wait for you to become a member of His family. And just as the Savior rejoiced that you became His follower, His heart longs to celebrate over your neighbor, your friend, and your family member. We know about the longing of Jesus' heart because He prayed for your salvation and then prayed you would be a part of telling the world about Him. "I am praying not only for these disciples but also for all who will ever believe in me through their message ... And may they be in us so that the world will believe you sent me" (John 17:20–21).

STEP TOWARD LIFE CHANGE
From *Reset: Why Discipleship Isn't About Trying Harder*
by Jeff Bogue

It was a huge crowd. The people were all waiting for someone to say something. So he stepped up and gave his first real sermon. It was a homerun! "Those who believed what Peter said were baptized and added to the church that day—about 3,000 in all" (Acts 2:41).

This was the real beginning of the church. On the day of Pentecost, the Holy Spirit filled the followers of Jesus and birthed a Jesus church movement that has lasted for more than two thousand years. It appears those early church leaders knew something about church growth that seems to elude most churches in the twenty-first century.

Today's church growth can sometimes be a mile wide and an inch deep. But the early church growth had spiritual depth because Jesus' followers had traded a legalistic religious theology for an experiential relational theology. These new Spirit-filled converts became committed disciples who shared an authentic and transformational faith with their neighbors and instilled that same faith into the next generation. Church historians say that from AD 100 to AD 300, the church exploded with spiritual growth, multiplying eight hundred times! That means, on average, the church quadrupled every generation for five consecutive generations. It grew from twenty-five thousand Christians in AD 100 to 20 million by AD 300! **And in the process, they changed the known world!**

The early Christians created a womblike atmosphere that was safe and conducive to answering questions, guiding discussion, and relationally being there for others to accept, encourage, support, and comfort. As a result, a sense of belonging and ownership was fostered, spiritual guidance was given and received, opportunities for service were seized, and accountability accepted. "And each day the Lord added to their fellowship those who were being saved" (Acts 2:47).

PRAY and Experience Scripture

Spend a few minutes in quiet prayer before the Lord. Ask God to speak to you, assuring Him of your willingness to hear His words and yield to His will. Ask Him to show you how He might want to change you so that you can more effectively meet the needs of other people, just like those in the early church. Who might need your acceptance, encouragement, support, or comfort? Be sure to including your family, friends, church members, and those who do not know Christ in your assessment. Ask Jesus to reveal how He might want to change your approach to ministry.

Review this list of ten needs as you pray. Does God want you to become . . .

- more accepting?
- more affectionate?
- more appreciative?
- more approving?
- more attentive?

- more comforting?
- more encouraging?
- more respectful?
- more committed to the security of others?
- more supportive?

Jesus, show me how I need to change. Speak to me, Lord, I am listening…

When it comes down to it, this idea of transforming a dead person in sin into a brand-new person who can live forever is the stuff of miracles. It can't happen otherwise. Notice what the disciples asked when Jesus said it was nearly impossible for a rich man who relies on his own riches to make it to heaven: "'Then who in the world can be saved?'… Jesus looked at them intently and said, 'Humanly speaking, it is impossible. But with God everything is possible'" (Matthew 19:25–26).

That's really the point, isn't it? Jesus is either the miracle worker and our only hope, or He's not. He is either God and can forgive us because of His sacrificial death, or He isn't and He can't. So we all have a choice to make. To place our trust in Christ's death as our ransom out of slavery to sin and death requires that we make a choice to turn our backs on our self-effort and our self-reliant life and accept his miracle-working power to give us eternal life.

LEARN to Encounter Jesus

Take the next few moments to reflect on the story of your personal decision for Christ. Think back to the time when Jesus transformed you from a dead person in sin into a brand-new creation. Think about *how* you were brought to salvation. Did the Spirit reveal Christ through Scripture? Was Christ revealed through the testimony of the changed lives around you? Did He reveal Himself to you directly? How did you come to know Him, and what changed about your life?

Christ was revealed to me through _____

And that changed the way I…

(For example: Christ was revealed to me through the gracious example of my grandfather. I received Christ as my Lord, and that changed my rebellious heart. I began pursuing Him.)

Thank God for your salvation and ask Him to bring more change to your life. "So then, just as you received Christ Jesus as Lord, continue to live … in him" (Colossians 2:6 NIV).

God, thank You for revealing Your Son to me. I praise You for the grace that has brought countless blessings to me. Please continue to reveal Yourself to me as I continue to yield myself to You.

In the past I tried to motivate people to trust in Christ out of fear. You know the drill: "If you want to avoid hell, turn to Jesus." But Jesus is not the great condemner; He is the great lover. And I began to see that if I could just help people grasp how much he loves them, they would repent of their self-effort and sin and turn to him. But, of course, that approach won't work unless and until we personally see just how much of a great lover God is.

I've found it is a mistake to rush or push people into a superficial prayer of forgiveness. It is better that they understand what Christ had to do and how he wants a relationship with them. Some time ago, I stopped asking people to pray a sinner's prayer until they really understood what they were repenting of. If the Holy Spirit isn't drawing a person to Jesus, and if that person doesn't see the need to repent, reciting a prayer isn't going to do much.

Leading people to Christ is really the role of a matchmaker. We merely introduce them to the One Person who wants an intimate love relationship for all eternity. God wants to reflect to seekers his love, kindness, and patience through matchmakers like you and me. I can *tell* people how much God loves them and wants a relationship with them, but my matchmaking will be much more effective if I am a living witness of that love. It is ultimately the Holy Spirit who must actually draw people to Jesus. And when the Holy Spirit is working through us, urging the seeker to respond to God's heart of love, that's when you and I can lead them to a relationship with Jesus.

SHARE with Others in Community

"As each one has received a special gift, employ it in serving one another as good stewards of the manifold grace of God." (1 Peter 4:10 NASB)

Consider, for a moment, the "manifold" or "multifaceted" grace of God. God's grace has, at times, been expressed toward you in these ways (or facets):

- Acceptance when you have failed (Romans 15:7).

- Encouragement when you were down
  (1 Thessalonians 5:11).
- Support when you have struggled (Galatians 6:2).

Plan to share this story with another person. Talk about the ways that Jesus' grace has changed your life. Your words might begin like this:

God's grace is amazing because it changed me! God showed a specific aspect of His grace to me when _____ and I changed...

LOVE Others in Community

Now, pause to ask God this question: "God, how could I better express Your grace to others?"

Ask Him specifically about these aspects of His grace—acceptance, encouragement, and support.

Listen—and be still. Allow God's Spirit to reveal who needs to receive His grace through you. Then complete the following sentences.

I could better express God's . . .
- *acceptance to* _____.
- *encouragement to* _____.
- *support to* _____.

For example: I could better express God's support to my boss. He seems overwhelmed with all the demands at work. I could lighten his load by offering to help meet the deadline he is facing.

18

Equip me as I impart faith to the children who are in my care. I stand ready to fulfill my calling as a disciple-maker in their lives.

Jesus, reset my prayer life.

Children are precious in the sight of Jesus. While they may be little in size, Jesus thinks children are a big deal. Remember Matthew 19:13, where we read, "Then little children were brought to Him that He might put His hands on them and pray" (NKJV). And then, despite the fact that "the disciples rebuked" those who brought them, Jesus said the children should not be ushered away, "for the kingdom of heaven belongs to such as these" (v. 14 NIV). Wouldn't you have loved to listen in as Christ prayed for the children that day? Wouldn't it have been fun to hear what Jesus prayed for your child's future or His hopes for the days ahead? As Jesus resets our prayer life, may we fall in line with His prayer for us.

PREPARING YOUR CHILD FOR THE ROAD LEAST TRAVELED

From *Parenting with Intimacy* by Terri Snead

As you cradled your soft, rosy-cheeked newborn in your arms, do you remember what you were thinking? No doubt there were thoughts of amazement and adoration and perhaps a little apprehension. You certainly weren't thinking, "Precious gift of God, I want you to know that your dependency upon me is only temporary. My God-given responsibility from this day forward is to prepare you to leave home." Sounds ridiculous, doesn't it? In that moment, you couldn't imagine *ever* turning loose that bundle of joy. And yet, that's exactly your mission: to daily build into your child's life, to equip her to one day chart her own course as she moves out into the world. That's your role: to equip your child to leave spiritually confident, optimistic, and hopeful about what God has in store for his or her future.

PRAY and Experience Scripture

"Call to me and I will answer you…" (Jeremiah 33:3 NIV)

If you're like most of us, you may be feeling the pressure and weightiness of this role! This is a perfect time to invite God into the challenges of our calling. Let's do as this passage says: let's call on Him, confident that He will answer. Spend the next few moments calling upon Jesus. Tell Him of your needs and then listen for His answer.

> Jesus, I feel _____ when I think about my role as the primary disciple-maker of my kids. I'm calling on You to guide me in...
> And I'm listening for Your answer...

It sounds counterintuitive, but parents who are serious about living out their calling as disciple-makers must selflessly take care of themselves. Think about the flight attendant's instructions that are given to every parent traveling with small children: "If the cabin should lose pressure, your oxygen mask will drop from the ceiling. Be sure to put on your own mask before attending to your child." The same principle holds true in disciple-making. If you want to pass along God's love, grace, and compassion to your kids, you must experience these first yourself. If you want to impart a faith that's vibrant, relevant, and meaningful, pursue that kind of faith on your own. Make faith a priority and then out of gratitude for God's work in your own life, share the same with your kids.

As you focus on taking care of yourself as a parent, if you're married, be sure to make it a priority to keep your marriage strong. As your child sees the strength of your marriage relationship, it gives him or her the freedom to grow up and the foundation to embrace a relationship with Jesus. If Mom and Dad's marriage is strong—not perfect, but strong—that gives the child permission to do the job that God has given them to do: grow spiritually, emotionally, and physically. And remember, no matter what your marital status, God has not called you to be a perfect parent with perfect kids. He has called you to be a faithful parent, equipping your children to become all they can be in Him.

Here's a next step in your pursuit of a vibrant, personal faith.

■ LEARN to Encounter Jesus

Pause and imagine yourself standing before your children—your gifts from the Lord. Each gift is uniquely packaged, preciously wrapped, and carefully presented.

As you admire your beautifully wrapped gifts, you look over your shoulder to see Jesus standing next to you.

Jesus leans forward to look more closely at your children and seems to gaze in awe of His creation. He smiles with satisfaction and approval. His eyes sparkle as He admires every aspect of these precious gifts. Speaking with admiration, the Master Creator reminds you of how He knows these children intimately; He formed them in the womb (Jeremiah 1:5). Jesus reminds you that He notices each part of their day—when they rise up and when they lie down (Psalm 139:1–3). Christ lovingly recalls how He knows and admires each child's gifts and talents (Psalm 139:14–16). Jesus offers reassurance that He hears each child's thoughts and intentions and knows the intricacies of their character (Psalm 139:23). Jesus leaves your side, but before He does, He whispers an invitation: "Will you join me? Let's work together to unwrap these gifts. Will you join me in knowing these children so intimately that we can admire how special they are together?"

Now voice your prayer to Jesus. Tell Him that you want to have the Creator's perspective.

Jesus, when I look at my children, I want to see what You see. Give me Your eyes to see their unique beauty. Give me Your ears to hear their needs. Give me Your heart of approval for them. I want to join You in loving them well.

A divine perspective is critical to our missional role as parents because effective disciple-makers are always careful to affirm a child's identity. These parents intentionally confirm the identity that God has declared to be truth about their children. Affirming a child's identity means understanding who God has created them to be and what the Scriptures say about who they are in God's eyes. Scripture teaches three essential truths that will lead your child to embrace an accurate view of how God sees her.

- **I am created in God's image.** Children need our confirmation that they did not simply descend or ascend from the monkeys or the slime of the ocean. They are a special creation, made in the likeness of God.
- **I am fallen but not worthless.** Our children need constant reminders that (just like their moms and dads), they are fallen and sinful, but they are also worth the gift of God's Son. Our works are worthless; we are not.
- **I am supremely and sacrificially loved.** Our children need affirmation of how much they are loved and to what lengths God was willing to go in order to show them He cares. God has entrusted you with His precious "gifts." Let Him remind you to cherish these gifts.

As you help your child navigate this busy, craze-filled world, be careful not to miss some of the real secrets of how to be a successful disciple-maker. Don't let *good things* distract you from the *best things*.

George Mueller, a nineteenth-century minister, orphanage director, and author was asked about his secrets for success. He answered, "As I look back on my life, what I see is that I was constantly brought to crossroads in my life—crossroads which demanded a choice of which way I should go. As I was brought to those crossroads, I believe the key to my success is that I seemed to have consistently chosen the least traveled path."

There's a broad road for parenting. It's a wide path where many travel. Let's be sure to model a vibrant faith of our own so that we're equipped to affirm a child's God-given identity and then launch them onto the road least traveled.

SHARE with Others in Community

An important aspect of spiritual legacy includes spiritual conversations. First, plan to have a spiritual conversation with your child. Then talk to another adult about Jesus and how He has made a difference in your parenting. Your words might begin with these:

> With child: Jesus has given me the incredible job of being your mom/dad. I take that job seriously, and so I am asking Jesus to help me...
> With adult: I have a new perspective on my parenting. Instead of just trying to get along with my kids, I'm trying to see them with the eyes of Jesus. It's made a huge difference in...

LOVE Others in Community

Look for ways to see your children with the eyes of Jesus. Give them your undivided attention.

Look for ways to hear with the ears of Jesus. Listen to their words and the needs behind them. Listen with a desire to know them more deeply.

19

We want to see more Spirit-empowered churches where there is a focus on evangelism, practical service to those in need, more evident giving among believers, and well-being among church members is evident to everyone.

Jesus, reset my prayer life.

In Jesus' great prayer, He explained, "And this is eternal life, that they may know You, the only true God, and Jesus Christ whom You have sent" (John 17:3 NASB). Paul perfectly understood this goal and privilege. To the believers in Philippi, he related that no power, prestige, or wealth could compete with the thrill of knowing God. Compared to the wonder and joy of his relationship with God, everything else was only "rubbish" (Philippians 3:7–9 NASB). Perhaps this contrast is important as we pray toward the goal of Spirit-empowered churches. Could we start with knowing Him rather than doing for Him? Perhaps we should set aside working toward powerful churches, prestigious churches, or wealthy churches and instead work toward knowing Jesus more intimately.

A SPIRIT-EMPOWERED CHURCH: AN ACTS 2 MINISTRY MODEL

From A *Spirit-Empowered Church: An Acts 2 Ministry Model*
by Alton Garrison

If you ask a variety of people across denominational lines the purpose of the Holy Spirit in the church, you will get a wide range of answers. I believe the strongest doctrinal case for the purpose of Spirit-empowerment is carrying out the transformative mission of God among both the unchurched and stagnant, uninspired believers. With the challenges facing the church today, we cannot rely on our own ingenuity, intellect, and human effort. God has not abandoned us to that fruitless recourse; but when we take hold of the Spirit as power, He fully equips and emboldens us to present hope to a lost world.

The Holy Spirit helps us to be more than we are. He empowers us, and the same Spirit that rested on a murderer, turning him into a deliverer; on a shepherd boy, turning him into a king; and on a long-haired womanizer, turning him into a judge, does not momentarily "rest" upon us. The Holy Spirit stayed with fishermen and turned them into disciples. He converted a religious murderer, indwelled him, and enabled him to write much of the New Testament. And most notably, the Spirit lived in and through a carpenter who was the Savior of the world. He empowers every believer who accepts His saving grace and humbly makes himself available to be used by God.

The Holy Spirit will also help you say more than you know. Emboldened by the Holy Spirit, Peter may be the best example of this. Right after the Spirit fell in the upper room, he stood up from among the eleven disciples, raised his voice, and addressed the crowd in a Spirit-inspired speech. The results were nothing short of miraculous; they baptized and added three thousand people to the church that day. The Holy Spirit helped Peter beyond his ability, and the listeners went from wondering what it could mean that the believers were speaking in other tongues to asking, "What should we do?" to receiving Christ. That same inspiration and empowerment are what enable us to share the gospel effectively.

The Holy Spirit also helps us do more than we can. Before commissioning us to share the gospel, Jesus promised us power. He said, "But you shall receive power when the Holy Spirit has come upon you; and you shall be witnesses to Me in Jerusalem, and in all Judea and Samaria, and to the end of the earth" (Acts 1:8). The Spirit's power is the fulfillment of Jesus' promise that those who believe in Him would do the same works He did … and even greater. Examples of God's power encourage us to believe for the supernatural. After the Holy Spirit fell, the disciples performed many miracles, including but not limited to healing the sick, casting out demons, and discipling untold thousands. And unlike Spirit-touched heroes of the Old Testament who momentarily enjoyed His power, the believers in the Acts 2 church experienced the lingering, indwelling power of the Holy Spirit.

LEARN to Encounter Jesus

"[Out of your] innermost being shall flow rivers of living water." (John 7:38 NASB)

Quietly meditate on the invitation of Jesus. Imagine that He is standing before you. His eyes are kind and welcoming. His heart is tender and yet affirming. He stands before you with these words of invitation: "I've given you My Spirit to live inside you. The power of the living God can transform you, embolden your speech, and empower your witness. You have the power. You have the boldness. You have the words. Now let my Spirit flow out of you like rivers of living water." Welcome the Holy Spirit's prompting and empowerment. Thank the Lord Jesus for not leaving you alone, but coming to you through His Spirit.

Jesus, I receive all that the Spirit has given me…

I am thankful for the gift of the Holy Spirit, especially because…

BUILDING ON A FIRST-CENTURY BLUEPRINT

The first-century church was founded in prayer. In Acts 1, we read that Jesus' church development core team consisted of Peter, James, and John (the big three), the rest of the remaining disciples, His mother and brothers, and several women who helped support His earthly ministry. They all joined together in prayer. The results of this prayer and founding blueprint were nothing short of miraculous.

Imagine these things being true in each of our churches: the church received the Holy Spirit willingly, demonstrated power supernaturally, was led effectively, prayed fervently, fellowshipped regularly, taught sound doctrine consistently, preached the gospel passionately, shared resources liberally, and *grew exponentially*. This last result was a consequence of all those factors that preceded it.

We read that they had a sense of awe as they saw the Spirit move on the disciples, enabling them to perform miraculous signs and wonders. (And if you do not think that sharing their property, possessions, and finances with those in need was a miracle, you try it!) Their days consisted of worshipping together, sharing meals with great joy and generosity, praising God, and enjoying the goodwill of their community. And as they lived out this organic, Spirit-empowered life, God exploded their numbers.

PRAY and Experience Scripture

The book of Acts describes several important characteristics of the early church. These defining traits enabled that body of believers to impact their world in an astounding way. Read over the characteristics identified below and explore the accompanying Scripture passages:

- They were devoted to teaching the Word of God (Acts 2:42).
- They were devoted to fellowship with other believers (v. 42).
- They were devoted to prayer (v. 42).
- They had a reputation for unity (v. 44).
- They were generous toward those in need (v. 44).

- Others took note that they had been with Jesus (4:13).
- They were willing to speak the Word of God with boldness (v. 31).
- They were of one heart and mind (v. 32).
- They gave witness of Christ with great power as abundant grace was upon them (v. 33).
- People held them in high esteem (5:13).
- Through Spirit-prompted ministry, multitudes were constantly being added to the kingdom (v. 14).
- They rejoiced at being considered worthy to suffer shame in Jesus' name (v. 41).

As you read each Scripture, pause to listen for God's prompting. Ask Him to help you answer the following questions:

- Which of these characteristics are most true of my life?
- Which ones may need to be restored in my life?
- Which of these characteristics are most true of my ministry?
- Which ones may need to be restored in my ministry?

Be still before the Lord as you reflect on these questions. Then complete the following sentences:

Lord, please show me what characteristics you want to see more of in my life and in my ministry.

What Empowerment Is and Is Not

Experiencing a Spirit-empowered church means understanding that our relationship with Christ goes beyond mere belief or the washing away of sins. (These are the means through which Christ makes a relationship possible, but a life of following Him and knowing Him intimately yet awaits.) It is not about doing more for God, performing at a higher level, or even experiencing signs and wonders. It is about knowing Him.

SHARE with Others in Community

"We are therefore Christ's ambassadors, as though God were making his appeal through us…" (2 Corinthians 5:20 NIV)

Consider again Christ's startling love at Calvary: He forgave those who had wounded Him. He accepted a thief before he had changed. He supported His own mother, even while suffering excruciating pain and sacrificing Himself.

Remember Christ's loving initiative of forgiveness, acceptance, and support. Then pause to review the people whom God has placed in your life. You have been placed there as His ambassador. Jesus longs to share His love through you.

Who among your family, friends, coworkers, and acquaintances could benefit from:

- His forgiveness through you (no matter what their sin)?
- His acceptance through you (even before they change)?
- His support through you (even if they have not asked)?

✝ Share your responses (with specific names) with a prayer partner. Pray together, asking the Spirit to remove hindrances to your witness and to empower the sharing of God's startling love.

→ **LOVE** Others in Community

Make plans to demonstrate God's forgiveness, acceptance, and support to the people He has revealed to you. Tell your prayer partner about these plans as a step of accountability.

20

*We want to see young adults,
students, and children embracing
the claims of Christ.
Please do Your miraculous work
so that more young people live
and love like Jesus.*

Jesus, reset my prayer life.

With all the bad news reported about young adults, college students, and youth, it might feel overwhelming to pray for revival and awakening in this generation. We must ask ourselves this question, though: "Is this how Jesus thinks about youth and young adults?" Scripture reveals the answer. Jesus most certainly didn't dismiss the needs of the youth; He actually prioritized the youngest ones in His miracles, His interactions, and even His sermons. "So anyone who becomes as humble as this little child is the greatest in the Kingdom of Heaven" (Matthew 18:4). We see an additional evidence of Jesus' perspective in His prayer of thanksgiving: "O Father, Lord of heaven and earth, thank you for hiding these things from those who think themselves wise and clever, and for revealing them to the childlike" (Matthew 11:25). As we dig past the surface, there are many reasons to give us hope to pray fervently for the younger generations and expect God to move among them.

YOUTH *ISN'T* WASTED ON THE YOUNG

From the article "Youth Isn't Wasted on the Young"

by Jeremy Story

It's important to remember Christ's perspective on young adults, but we also can't deny the significant contributions that students have made to the spiritual climate of our nation. Did you know that the outreach and missions movement of our country can be traced back to the prayers and actions of college students? In 1806, five students gathered regularly to pray at Williams College in Massachusetts. On one occasion during a rainstorm, they took refuge under a haystack and God directly impressed on them the vision to reach the world. Afterward, it was several of these same students who helped start the first missions-sending agency in America!

Later in 1886, at a college conference again in Massachusetts, one hundred students from campuses across America committed their lives to go overseas. This commitment developed into the Student Volunteer Movement, which sent more than twenty thousand missionaries overseas with sixty thousand other Americans praying for them and supporting them.

Did you know that God responded to prayer specifically for the youth during the tumultuous sexual revolution in the late 1960s? In the 1970s, the Jesus Movement spread throughout the hippie culture (the student and young adult population) and then throughout our nation. Students came to Jesus—*the One who is love*—right out of the free love movement. Additionally, our modern version of Christian worship music was born out of this movement of youth. And in 1971, a psychedelic tie-dye drawing of Jesus graced the front cover of *Time* magazine in recognition of the culture shift.

In 1963, the Supreme Court outlawed prayer led by staff within public schools, and in 1964, the required Bible reading was also outlawed. However, by the 1990s, millions of high school, middle school, and even elementary students gathered to pray around the flagpoles of their campuses. Students continue to lead the way despite the country's shift away from prayer and biblical absolutes.

Our country is filled with evidences of how far we have moved from God, but our students continue to uphold the things that matter to God. For instance, it is true to say that abortion has had a devastating effect on our nation. Since 1973, 58 million unborn babies have died. Yet God raised up youth, college students, and young adults who are committed to changing this trend in our country. In 2000, approximately four hundred thousand students gathered for *The Call*, a national solemn assembly of students at the National Mall in Washington, DC. Out of this movement, rallying moments of prayer and mobilizing action have been able to turn the tide of abortion in our nation. Pictures of these students have filled the media. They pray boldly, but they pray silently. The students silently pray while wearing red tape over their mouths with the word *Life* inscribed across it. As a result, while public policy still allows abortion, most every media outlet and policy poll has noted a decline in the number of abortions and a decrease in the cultural popularity of abortion.

LEARN to Encounter Jesus

Imagine that you are one of the teenagers standing in the crowd listening to Jesus. You've overheard the teacher confirm the incredible stories that have been told throughout Galilee. "The blind see, the lame walk, the lepers are cured, the deaf hear, the dead are raised to life, and the Good News is being preached to the poor" (Matthew 11:5). You're awestruck by the great things that these adults have done. You wonder if God could ever include a young person as He advances His kingdom. And then you hear something incredible. Jesus bows His head and prays. His prayer gives a perspective you've never heard before. "O Father, Lord of heaven and earth, thank you for hiding these things from those who think themselves wise and clever, and for revealing them to the childlike" (Matthew 11:25). Your heart is full because you realize that Christ doesn't just value a certain age or stage of life. He values the teachable heart. Jesus is grateful any time that you come to Him with youthlike faith. Declare that faith now:

Jesus, I am grateful that Your values are often different than the world's values. Thank You for receiving me any time that I am humble and teachable. I am ready for You to reveal any changes that You might want for my life. Speak, Lord, I am listening.

From the First Great Awakening to the Jesus Movement, youth have played a key role in instigating and sustaining works of God. We have tremendous reason and hope to pray for our young adults, college students, and youth. Here are some great and simple ways you can pray for them.

PRAY and Experience Scripture

"If you believe, you will receive whatever you ask for in prayer" (Matthew 21:22 NIV). Pray the following prayers with boldness, believing that you will receive what you ask. You can be certain that these needs are according to His will. Therefore, in boldness, make your requests known to God:

Pray for the workers first, not the harvest first. Jesus said, "The harvest is plentiful, but the workers are few. Ask the Lord of the harvest, therefore, to send out workers into his harvest field" (Luke 10:2 NIV). The problem isn't with people who don't yet know Jesus; it is with the number of Christians willing to share Jesus in bold word and deed. Pray for God to send out workers into the ripe harvest that is already present among youth and young adults.

Jesus, raise up workers who have a passion for young people and who are ready, able, and committed to telling students and young adults about you. Lord, I pray for an abundance of "workers"—not just a few!

Pray for the adult influencers and leaders. College professors are notorious for taking pride in "enlightening" students by challenging them to abandon a life centered on faith in God. Pray especially then for God's favor on those professors who are taking a firm stand and who share publically about their faith and in their field of study. Pray also for public school teachers. Pray that they would be "as shrewd as snakes and as innocent as doves" (Matthew 10:16 NIV) so they can live out their faith in Jesus strongly while doing their jobs well.

> Jesus, I pray for the teachers' protection and their boldness to live out their faith with strength and power. I believe You can reclaim education for Your glory!

Pray for purity. One of the biggest tempters and thieves of future destinies among youth and young adults is sexual impurity. Never before has there been such sexual and gender confusion in our nation. Therefore, pray that sexual purity will be valued among our youth and that they will actively pursue lifelong sexual relationships in marriage. Pray that youth will reject the destructive lies fed to them by popular culture and resist the message that freedom means not being "tied down" to one person sexually. Pray that students will be bold and patiently wait for their spouse. Ask God to direct our youth and young adults away from the confusion and temptation that is so prevalently proclaimed in movies, books, television, news, and music. One generation "turned on" the sexual revolution, and another generation can turn it off.

> Jesus, I pray for the purity of our young people. Let them see the lies of the world with clarity and then empower their pursuit of relationships that are pure. Make the standard of lifelong sexual relationships in marriage attractive again. Create a hunger in our young people for the "good things" that You desire for them. May they settle for nothing less.

Pray for unity. One of Jesus' last prayers on earth was that we would be one as He and the Father were one, so that the world would know He was God (John 17:23). Pray that this next generation of leaders embraces a kingdom mentality that doesn't compete but collaborates to proclaim Jesus.

✚ SHARE with Others in Community

Talk to another church, ministry, or community leader about your desire to make an impact on the next generation. Tell them how Jesus has begun to reset your perspective. Talk about your desire for unity and collaboration.

Jesus has begun to reset my perspective on reaching students and young adults. He has specifically spoken to me about…

➡ LOVE Others in Community

Look for a student or young adult who could benefit from your care. Does this person need a family connection? Does this student need support with their work/class requirements? Is there a student who might need a mentor or coach for their relationships?

Jesus, show me a student or young adult who could benefit from my demonstration of care. Show me, Lord. I'm listening…

ABOUT THE AUTHORS AND THEIR RESOURCES

JOE BATTAGLIA

Excerpt from: **The Politically Incorrect Jesus: Living Boldly in a Culture of Unbelief**

Copyright © 2015 by Joe Battaglia

Used by permission of BroadStreet Publishing Group. www.broadstreetpublishing.com

ISBN: 978-1424549818

To purchase the full resource: www.thepoliticallyincorrectjesus.com

ABOUT THE AUTHOR:

Joe Battaglia is the founder and president of Renaissance Communications (www.renn.com), a media company specializing in the production and syndication of radio programming, media consulting, and creative promotions. He still lives in New Jersey, and can be found at times hanging around street corners with old friends singing doo-wop songs, because that is where Jesus might be if He were around today.

• • • • •

MARK BATTERSON

Excerpt from: **The Circle Maker**

Copyright © 2011 by Mark Batterson.

Used by permission of Zondervan. www.zondervan.com

The Circle Maker, Praying Circles Around Your Biggest Dreams and Greatest Fears gives insight and clarity about the importance of "dreaming big, praying hard and thinking long."

ABOUT THE AUTHOR:

Mark Batterson is the New York Times bestselling author of *The Circle Maker*, *The Grave Robber*, and *A Trip around the Sun*. He is the lead pastor of National Community Church, one church with seven campuses in Washington, DC. Mark has a doctor of ministry degree from Regent University and lives on Capitol Hill with his wife, Lora, and their three children. Learn more at www.markbatterson.com.

• • • • •

JEFFREY A. BOGUE
Excerpt from: **RESET: Why Discipleship Isn't About Trying Harder**
Copyright © 2013 by Jeffrey A. Bogue
Publisher: Living Naked Press
Akron, Ohio 44333
ISBN-13: 978-1628905182
To purchase this complete book: https://www.store.graceohio.org

ABOUT THE AUTHOR:

In 1993, Jeff Bogue and his wife, Heidi, accepted the position of youth ministers at Grace Church in Akron, Ohio. After building a successful youth ministry of over 300 youth, Jeff and Heidi accepted the challenge of pastoring a new campus of Grace Church, starting with under 200 people and the support of the Akron Grace mother church. Today, Jeff serves as senior pastor, leading multiple campuses and church plants with over 7,000 people calling Grace their home.

Jeff's story isn't about his pastoral skills or leadership; it's about his struggles to overcome his misconceptions of God, himself, and his role in discipling people to maturity in Christ. You will find his story inspiring, challenging, and instructional in raising up committed followers of Jesus through the relational heart of God. Dr. Bogue and his wife, Heidi, have been married twenty-two years and have six children.

. . . . .

DAVE BUTTS
Excerpt from: **Forgotten Power: A Simply Theology for a Praying Church**
Copyright © 2015 by Dave Butts
Publisher: Prayer Shop Publishing, Terre Haute, IN
Used by permission.

ABOUT THE AUTHOR:

Dave is President of Harvest Prayer Ministries. He also serves the Kingdom in the following positions: President, Gospel Revivals, Inc. (Herald of His Coming); Chairman, America's National Prayer Committee; Facilitation Committee - Mission America Coalition; Executive Committee - Awakening America Alliance; President 2014 - International Conference on Missions (ICOM).

Besides authoring numerous magazine articles on prayer and missions for various publications, Dave is the author of: Forgotten Power; When God Shows Up: Essays on Revival; and, Pray Like the King: Lessons from the Prayers of Israel's Kings, which he wrote jointly with his wife, Kim. To purchase resources: www.prayershop.org. For scheduling, contact: dave@harvestprayer.com.

RONNIE FLOYD
Excerpt from: ***Power of Prayer and Fasting***
Publisher: B&H Books; Second edition
ISBN: 978-0805464832

ABOUT THE AUTHOR:

www.RonnieFloyd.com.

Follow him on Twitter @RonnieFloyd and Instagram @RonnieFloyd

Ronnie Floyd was elected president of the Southern Baptist Convention in 2014 and is pastor of Cross Church in NW Arkansas, a multi-site fellowship of believers. From a desire to influence the vibrant Northwest Arkansas business community, he founded the Northwest Arkansas Business Persons Summit. Additionally, he also founded the Cross Church School of Ministry, a one-year ministry residency that prepares leaders for life, ministry, and gospel advancement globally. Currently, he is the general editor of LifeWay's Bible Studies for Life, and author of over 20 books.

∘ ∘ ∘ ∘ ∘

STEVE GAINES
Excerpt from: ***Pray Like It Matters***
Publisher: Auxano Press (June 15, 2013)
www.auxanopress.com
ISBN-13: 978-0988985421

ABOUT THE AUTHOR:

Steve Gaines: A man of prayer and a preacher of God's Word, Dr. Steve Gaines pastored churches in Texas, Tennessee, and Alabama since 1983, before following Adrian Rogers at Bellevue Baptist Church, Memphis, in 2005 as Senior Pastor. He has served on many denominational boards and committees, most notably the Baptist Faith and Message Study Committee. He was president of the Southern Baptist Pastors Conference in 2005 and has been keynote speaker at many denominational events. He is the author of two books, *Morning Manna* and *When God Comes to Church*. Steve and his wife, Donna, have four children and four grandchildren.

∘ ∘ ∘ ∘ ∘

ALTON GARRISON

Excerpt from: **A Spirit-Empowered Church: An Acts 2 Ministry Model**

Publisher: Influence Resources (September 1, 2015)

ISBN: 978-1681540016

Find the full resource at:

www.amazon.com/Spirit-Empowered-Church-Acts-Ministry-Model/dp/1681540010

ABOUT THE AUTHOR:

Alton Garrison serves as the Assistant General Superintendent of the Assemblies of God. In addition, he serves as the director of the Acts 2 Revitalization Initiative, which helps churches renew their spiritual vitality and reach their full kingdom potential. He is the author of Hope in America's Crisis; Building the Winning Team; Acts 2 Church; and The 360° Disciple. Garrison and his wife, Johanna, currently reside in Springfield, Missouri.

• • • • •

STEVE HAWTHORNE

Excerpt from: **Toward Neighborhood Transformation: How to Live in a Prayed-For Neighborhood**

ABOUT THE AUTHOR:

Steve Hawthorne leads a prayer and mission mobilization group called WayMakers. Steve and his wife, Barbara, live in Austin, Texas. They have three children. He is widely known as the co-editor of the book and course called Perspectives on the World Christian Movement. Every year hundreds of churches use his prayer guide called Seek God for the City. You can contact WayMakers for printed copies @ www.waymakers.org, but also consider downloading this prayer guide to your mobile device. Steve speaks and writes with living passion for the greater glory of Jesus among the nations. Steve says of his work, "I like to commit arson of the heart."

Download **Seek God 2016** (January, 2016) for iOS on the App Store, for Android on Google Play, or for Kindle Fire at the Amazon Appstore. Just $0.99 cents. www.waymakers.org/pray/seek-god/app/

• • • • •

BISHOP HARRY JACKSON with RAPHAEL GREEN
Excerpt from blogs posts and articles from www.thereconciledchurch.org, featuring the Seven Bridges of Peace. Contact The Reconciled Church at reconciled@thehopeconnection.org.

ABOUT THE AUTHOR:
Harry R. Jackson Jr., is an African-American Christian preacher and Pentecostal bishop who serves as the senior pastor at Hope Christian Church in Beltsville, Maryland, and serves as a regional bishop in the Fellowship of International Churches. He is also a social conservative activist and commentator. Jackson is the founder and chairman of the High Impact Leadership Coalition, which is composed of ministers who actively promote socially conservative causes.

•••••

DR. MICHAEL LEWIS and DR. MARK DANCE
Excerpt from blog posts by Dr. Michael Lewis and Dr. Mark Dance. Blogs can be found at: mlewis.pastorforpastorsblog.com and www.lifeway.com/pastors.

ABOUT THE AUTHORS:
Dr. Michael Lewis serves as the Executive Director of Pastoral Care and Development of the North American Mission Board. The Pastor for Pastors' initiative he leads is a ministry that simply encourages and comes alongside pastors and their families. Michael has served as a pastor of local churches for 23 years in South Carolina, Georgia, Texas and Florida. In each of his pastorates, the church experienced spiritual and numerical growth resulting in the revitalization of a plateaued or declining condition.

Dr. Mark Dance is the Associate Vice President for Pastoral Leadership at LifeWay Christian Resources. Mark served as the Senior Pastor of Second Baptist Church in Conway, Arkansas, from 2001 to 2014. A native of Tyler, Texas, Mark pastored a church in San Antonio, Texas, and in Church Hill, Tennessee, before moving to Arkansas. Mark earned his undergraduate degree in business from Howard Payne University, an M.Div. from Southwestern Baptist Theological Seminary, and a D.Min. from the Southern Baptist Theological Seminary.

•••••

JOSH MCDOWELL

Excerpt from: **10 WAYS TO SAY "I LOVE YOU"**

Publisher: Harvest House Publishers

Eugene, Oregon 97402

www.harvesthousepublishers.com

Used by Permission

ISBN-13: 978-0736953870

To order complete book go to: www.josh.org

ABOUT THE AUTHOR:

Josh McDowell has been reaching the spiritually skeptical for more than five decades. Since beginning ministry in 1961, Josh has spoken to more than 25 million people in 128 countries. He is the author or coauthor of 148 books, with over 51 million copies distributed worldwide, including *Straight Talk with Your Kids About Sex*, *Experience Your Bible*, *Evidence for the Historical Jesus*, *More Than a Carpenter*, and *The New Evidence That Demands a Verdict*, recognized by *World* magazine as one of the twentieth century's top-40 books. Josh continues to travel throughout the United States and countries around the world, helping young people and adults strengthen their faith and understanding of Scripture.

• • • • •

JEDD MEDEFIND

Excerpt from: ***Becoming Home: Adoption, Foster Care, and Mentoring—***
Living Out God's Heart for Orphans (Frames) by Barna Group; Jedd Medefind

Used by permission of Zondervan. www.zondervan.com

ISBN: 978-0310433378

ABOUT THE AUTHOR:

Desiring to spur transformation through the Church, Jedd serves as President of the Christian Alliance for Orphans. Jedd believes that love for orphans transforms. Both personally and through the example of countless others, he's seen that lives are turned upside-down when Christians reflect God's heart for orphans through adoption, foster care, and global orphan care.

Jedd has written many articles and four books, including *Upended* and *Four Souls*. His most recent book, *Becoming Home*, offers a short yet meaningful exploration of how families and communities can embrace vulnerable children with wisdom and love through adoption, foster care, mentoring, and more.

• • • • •   •

STORMIE OMARTIAN AND JACK HAYFORD

Excerpt from: ***The Power of a Praying Church***

Copyright © 2003 by Stormie Omartian and Jack Hayford

Publisher: Harvest House Publishers, Eugene, Oregon 97402

www.harvesthousepublishers.com

Used by permission.

ISBN-13: 978-0736920773

ABOUT THE AUTHORS:

Stormie Omartian is the best-selling author of The Power of a Praying series with over 32 million books sold worldwide. In high demand as an international speaker, Stormie's passion is to help people know God and love Him in a deep way. A survivor of child abuse, Stormie brings a deep understanding of recovery issues to her work.

In 2014, Stormie Omartian and her daughter-in-law, Paige Omartian, launched a new online community called, Omartian.net. This online community gives its members an opportunity to receive exclusive, members only content from Stormie and Paige. Request an invite when you visit: www.Omartian.net

Jack Hayford is the founding pastor of the Church On The Way in Van Nuys, California, and currently the chancellor of the King's College and Seminary in Los Angeles. A best-selling author and songwriter, Pastor Hayford has penned more than four dozen books and 600 hymns and choruses, including "Majesty." He and his wife, Anna, have four children and eleven grandchildren.

· · · · ·

DR. JARED PINGLETON

Excerpt from: ***Making Magnificent Marriages***

Publisher: Marriage Improvement Tools; 1.0 edition

Springfield, MO 65809

ISBN-13: 978-0989918909

www.RelationshipHealthScore.com

ABOUT THE AUTHOR:

Dr. Jared Pingleton serves as the Director of the Counseling Department at Focus on the Family. As a Clinical Psychologist and credentialed minister, Jared is dually trained in both psychology and theology and specializes in the theoretical and clinical integration of the two disciplines. In professional practice since 1977, Dr. Pingleton has had the privilege to work with thousands of individuals and couples to offer help, hope, and healing to the hurting.

In addition to his clinical practice, he has served on the pastoral staff of two large churches and has taught at several Christian colleges and seminaries. A popular speaker, Jared connects well with all types of audiences with a unique blend of warmth, wit, and wisdom.

•••••

SAMUEL RODRIGUEZ

Excerpt from: **The Lamb's Agenda: Why Jesus Is Calling You to a Life of Righteousness and Justice**

Publisher: Thomas Nelson (April 1, 2013)

ISBN: 978-1400204496

ABOUT THE AUTHOR:

Rev. Samuel Rodriguez is President of the National Hispanic Christian Leadership Conference, America's largest Hispanic Christian organization. Named by CNN as "The leader of the Hispanic Evangelical Movement" and by the San Francisco Chronicle as one of America's new evangelical leaders, Rodriguez is also the recipient of the Martin Luther King Jr. Award presented by the Congress on Racial Equality. A featured speaker in White House and congressional meetings, he has been featured, profiled, and quoted by such media outlets as the New York Times, Christianity Today, Washington Post, Wall Street Journal, Newsweek, Univision, Fox News, Time, and Ministries Today. Rodriguez is also the Senior Pastor of New Season Christian Worship Center in Sacramento, California.

•••••

TERRI SNEAD

Excerpt from: **Parenting with Intimacy**

Publisher: Relationship Press (1995)

ISBN: 1 56476 522

ABOUT THE AUTHOR:

Terri Snead is a teacher and conference speaker with a Master's degree in Counseling from Sam Houston State University. She leads the Training and Resources Division of the Great Commandment Network where she has coauthored numerous books with her father, Dr. David Ferguson. Terri is married to Wayne with whom she enjoys lots of time with their four kids and two grandkids. To order GCN's resources, go to: www.greatcommandment.net.

•••••

JEREMY STORY

Original article by Jeremy Story: **Youth Isn't Wasted on the Young**

Contact Jeremy at (512) 331-5991 or info@campusrenewal.org

facebook.com/campusrenewal

2222 Rio Grande St. Suite B-130 Austin, TX 78705

ABOUT THE AUTHOR:

Jeremy has a history of starting great collegiate ministry movements across our nation. A self-proclaimed "systems man," he seeks to hear from God how to more effectively reach college students for Christ. He is a firm believer that transforming campuses for Christ means changing our nation in a powerful way, and wants to join with Him in His plan.

⁕ ⁕ ⁕ ⁕ ⁕

DOUG STRINGER

Excerpt from a republished article in Oct 2014, from the originally written article in preparation for Houston Prayer Mountain where Houston area churches gathered in prayer, fasting, and worship for 40 Days in 1996.

ABOUT THE AUTHOR:

Doug Stringer is the founder and director of Turning Point Ministries International, an evangelism and discipleship ministry with outreaches to the Church and the secular world. Doug also founded Somebody Cares America/International to mobilize the Church across racial and denominational lines in unified efforts of prayer, compassion evangelism, disaster response, and leadership training; being a tangible expression of God's love in their communities.

Doug is also a sought-after speaker nationally and internationally, and is the author of numerous books including: It's Time to Cross the Jordan; Who's Your Daddy Now?; Born to Die; The Fatherless Generation; Somebody Cares, and Living Life Well.

To find out more about Doug Stringer or Somebody Cares please visit the websites at: www.DougStringer.com or www.SomebodyCares.org.

⁕ ⁕ ⁕ ⁕ ⁕

DR. MARK L. WILLIAMS

Excerpt from: ***The Praying Church Handbook,*** Volume II (Edited by P. Douglas Small)
Available from Alive Publications. www.alivepublications.org

ABOUT THE AUTHOR:

Dr. Mark L. Williams serves as General Overseer for the Church of God, the highest leadership role in the denomination. Elected to the post in 2012, Williams previously served as second assistant general overseer from 2008-2012. Prior to leading the Church of God on the Executive Committee, Williams was state overseer for California-Nevada and was a member of the International Executive Council. Williams began his ministerial career as an evangelist, traveling on the weekends while earning a degree from Lee University.

* * * * *

GEORGE WOOD

Excerpt from: **10 *Key Moments When Jesus Prayed***

Article source: http://georgeowood.com/10-key-moments-when-jesus-prayed/

ABOUT THE AUTHOR:

Since August 2007, George has been the General Superintendent of the General Council of the Assemblies of God in the United States of America (AG) and has been Chairman of the World Assemblies of God Fellowship, the largest Pentecostal denomination in the world, since 2008. He previously served as General Secretary of the AG from 1993 to 2007.

Before his election to national office in the AG, he was Assistant Superintendent of the Southern California District of the AG (1988–93). For 17 years he was pastor of Newport Mesa Church in Costa Mesa, California. From 1965 until 1971, he was Director of Spiritual Life and Student Life at Evangel University in Springfield, Missouri. Wood and his wife, Jewel, have a daughter and son.

* * * * *

THE NATIONAL PRAYER ACCORD

IN RECOGNITION OF:

- Our absolute dependence on God
- The moral and spiritual challenges facing our nation
- Our national need for repentance and divine intervention
- The covenants of prayer that God has answered throughout history
- Our great hope for a general awakening to the lordship of Christ, the unity of His Body, and the sovereignty of His Kingdom

WE STRONGLY URGE ALL CHURCHES AND FOLLOWERS OF JESUS IN AMERICA to unite in seeking the face of God through prayer and fasting, persistently asking our Father to send revival to the Church and spiritual awakening to our nation so that Christ's Great Commission might be fulfilled worldwide in our generation.

WE RESOLVE TO PROMOTE AS AN ONGOING "RHYTHM OF PRAYER". . .

Weekly . . . **In private or small group prayer meetings**

Monthly . . . **In local ministry prayer gatherings**

Quarterly . . . **In prayer gatherings among local ministries and groups**

Annually . . . **In prayer meetings designed to unite Christians nationally**

THE AWAKENING
AMERICA ALLIANCE

**has intentionally focused on uniting
hearts in prayer around the**
Twenty Indicators of Spiritual Awakening.

Awakening America Alliance

Let's join Jesus in praying for:

1. Increasing testimony of the manifest presence of God
2. Increased conversions and baptisms
3. Amplified participation in corporate as well as individual prayer, fasting, and other spiritual disciplines leading to more effective discipleship
4. A decrease in divorces and renewed commitment to marriage between a man and a woman in covenant relationship as God intends
5. Imparting faith to children and youth by equipping parents to become the primary disciple-makers of their children
6. A passionate pursuit among churches for the well-being of their cities through the planting of new congregations, benevolent ministries, practical service, and focused evangelism
7. Commitment to radical generosity as evidenced by compassion ministries and global missions
8. Improved health among ministers as evidenced by their joy, decreased resignations, healthy, loving relationships within their families, and an increased response among young people called to the ministry
9. Christians involved in bold witness accompanied by miracles, dramatic conversions, and Holy Spirit-empowered victories over evil
10. Heightened expressions of love and unity among all believers, as demonstrated by the unity of pastors and leaders
11. Breakdowns of racial, social, and status barriers as Christ's church celebrates together – Jesus!
12. A restoration of morality, ethical foundations and accountability among leaders of church and government, business and politics.

13. A transformation of society through the restoration of Christ's influence in the arts, media, and communications
14. Increased care for the hungry and homeless, the most vulnerable and needy
15. Young adults, students, and children embracing the claims and life-style of Christ through the witness of peers who live and love as Jesus
16. Community and national leaders seeking out the church as an answer to society's problems
17. Increased care for children as "gifts from the Lord" as the gospel addresses abortion, adoption, foster care, and child well-being
18. Restoration of righteous relations between men and women; decrease in divorce rates, cohabitation, same-sex relations, sexual abuse, sexual trafficking, out-of-wedlock children, and STDs
19. An awakening to the "fear of the Lord" rather than the approval of people, thus restoring integrity and credibility
20. Neighborhood transformation and an accompanying decrease of social ills through increased expressions of "loving your neighbor" in service, compassion, and unity

* * * * *

ABOUT THE GREAT COMMANDMENT NETWORK

The Great Commandment Network is an international collaborative network of strategic Kingdom leaders from the faith community, marketplace, education and care-giving fields who prioritize the powerful simplicity of the words of Jesus to love God, love others, and see others become His followers (Matthew 22:37-40, Matthew 28:19-20).

THE GREAT COMMANDMENT NETWORK IS SERVED THROUGH THE FOLLOWING:

Relationship Press – This team collaborates, supports, and joins together with churches, denominational partners, and professional associates to develop, print, and produce resources that facilitate ongoing Great Commandment ministry.

The Center for Relational Leadership – Their mission is to teach, train and mentor both ministry and corporate leaders in Great Commandment principles, seeking to equip leaders with relational skills so they might lead as Jesus led.

The Galatians 6:6 Retreat Ministry – This ministry offers a unique two-day retreat for ministers and their spouses for personal renewal and for reestablishing and affirming ministry and family priorities.

The Center for Relational Care (CRC) – The CRC provides therapy and support to relationships in crisis through an accelerated process of growth and healing, including Relational Care Intensives for couples, families, and singles.

For more information on how you, your church, ministry, denomination, or movement can be served by the Great Commandment Network write or call:

Great Commandment Network
2511 South Lakeline Blvd.
Cedar Park, Texas 78613
#800-881-8008
Or visit our website: www.GreatCommandment.net

A SPIRIT-EMPOWERED FAITH
Expresses Itself in Great Commission Living
Empowered by Great Commandment Love

begins with the end in mind:
The Great Commission calls us
to make disciples.

Therefore, go and make disciples of all the nations, baptizing them in
the name of the Father and the Son and the Holy Spirit. Teach these new
disciples to obey all the commands I have given you. And be sure of this:
I am with you always, even to the end of the age. (Matthew 28:19-20)

The ultimate goal of our faith journey is to relate to the person of Jesus, because it is our relational connection to Jesus that will produce Christlikeness and spiritual growth. This relational perspective of discipleship is required if we hope to have a faith that is marked by the Spirit's power.

Models of discipleship that are based solely upon what we *know* and what we *do* are incomplete, lacking the empowerment of a life of loving and living intimately with Jesus. **A Spirit-empowered faith is relational and impossible to realize apart from a special work of the Spirit.** For example, the Spirit-empowered outcome of "listening to and hearing God" implies relationship – it is both relational in focus and requires the Holy Spirit's power to live.

begins at the right place:
The Great Commandment calls us to
start with loving God and loving others.

"You must love the Lord your God with all your heart, all your soul,
and all your mind.' This is the first and greatest commandment.
A second is equally important: 'Love your neighbor as yourself.'
The entire law and all the demands of the prophets are
based on these two commandments." (Matthew 22:37-40)

Relevant discipleship does not begin with doctrines or teaching, parables or stewardship – but with loving the Lord with all your heart, mind, soul, and strength and then loving the people closest to you. Since Matthew 22:37-40 gives us the first and greatest commandment, *a Spirit-empowered faith starts where the Great Commandment tells us to start: A disciple must first learn to deeply love the Lord and to express His love to the "nearest ones"—his or her family, church, and community (and in that order).*

 embraces a relational process of Christlikeness.

Scripture reminds us that there are three sources of light for our journey – Jesus, His Word, and His people. The process of discipleship (or becoming more like Jesus) occurs as we relate intimately with each source of light.

Walk in the light while you can, so the darkness will not overtake you. (John 12:35)

Spirit-empowered discipleship will require a lifestyle of:
- Fresh encounters with Jesus (John 8:12)
- Frequent experiences of Scripture (Psalm 119:105)
- Faithful engagement with God's people (Matthew 5:14)

 can be defined with observable outcomes using a biblical framework.

The metrics for measuring Spirit-empowered faith or the growth of a disciple comes from Scripture and are organized/framed around four distinct dimensions of a disciple who serves.

Now these are the gifts Christ gave to the church: the apostles, the prophets, the evangelists, and the pastors and teachers. Their responsibility is to equip God's people to do his work and build up the church, the body of Christ. (Ephesians 4:11–12)

A relational framework for organizing Spirit-Empowered Discipleship)
utcomes draws from a cluster analysis of several Greek (*diakoneo, leitourgeo, douleuo*) and Hebrew words (*'abad, Sharat*) which elaborate on the Ephesians 4:12 declaration that Christ's followers are to be equipped for works of ministry or service. Therefore, the 40 Spirit-Empowered Faith Outcomes have been identified and organized around:

- Serving/loving the Lord – *While they were **ministering** to the Lord and fasting…* (Acts 13:2 NASB).[1]
- Serving/loving the Word – *But we will devote ourselves to prayer and to the **ministry** of the word* (Acts 6:4 NASB).[2]
- Serving/loving people – *…through love **serve** one another* (Galatians 5:13 NASB).[3]
- Serving/loving His mission – *Now all these things are from God, who reconciled us to Himself through Christ and gave us the **ministry** of reconciliation* (2 Corinthians 5:18 NASB).[4]

1 Ferguson, David L. *Great Commandment Principle*. Cedar Park, Texas: Relationship Press, 2013.

2 Ferguson, David L. *Relational Foundations*. Cedar Park, Texas: Relationship Press, 2004.

3 Ferguson, David L. *Relational Discipleship*. Cedar Park, Texas: Relationship Press, 2005.

4 "Spirit Empowered Outcomes," www.empowered21.com, Empowered 21 Global Council, http://empowered21.com/discipleship-materials/.